THE LAWS OF
STEEL

LIVING A LIFE OF RESILIENCE, CONFIDENCE AND PROSPERITY

RYUHO OKAWA

IRH PRESS

BOOKS
IRH PRESS
New York

ISBN 13: 978-1-942125-65-5
ISBN 10: 1-942125-65-8

Printed in Canada

First Edition
Second Printing

Cover Image: © zffoto/shutterstock.com

CONTENTS

CHAPTER ONE

The Mindset to Invite Prosperity

CHAPTER THREE

Fulfilling *Noblesse Oblige*

Creating People and Nations that Can Produce
Value and Contribute to the World

CHAPTER FOUR

Be Confident in Your Life

Build the Kingdom of the Mind and Spread the Design of the World's Future

CHAPTER FIVE

A Savior's Wish

Awakening to the Life of Service to the World

Life-Changing Words 5:
Abandon, If You Want to Protect 196

CHAPTER SIX

The Power to Make Miracles

Opening Your Future with a Transparent Mind,
the Practice of Love, and Prayer

This book is a compilation of the lectures, with additions, as listed on page 230.

PREFACE

This book will guide you to live a life with resilience and strength. I do not use difficult words; I give concrete and practical teachings with many examples that apply to people of different backgrounds.

Do you understand the importance of having faith? While you believe in the existence of God or Buddha, can you also accept that your life is based on the law of cause and effect?

Do you understand my severe criticism of the current public perception on politics where people only think about receiving things from the government?

Can you see how all people, in every nation, are living through the flow of international politics?

Furthermore, can you see that the last and largest world religion is building up its pillars, even as it is being hammered like red-hot steel?

Ryuho Okawa
Master and CEO of Happy Science Group
December 2019

Chapter ONE

THE MINDSET TO INVITE PROSPERITY

Lecture given on November 23, 2018
at Special Lecture Hall, Happy Science, Tokyo, Japan

1

Happiness and Prosperity Are Within You

My talks affect people's hearts differently
Depending on their state of mind

This chapter entitled, "The Mindset to Invite Prosperity," mainly talks on the idea or way of thinking to achieve prosperity. People need to relearn this type of topic every year or once every few years in one way or another; otherwise, it will be easily forgotten.

Depending on your state of mind or the circumstances in which you find yourself, you might not absorb the essence of my talk, but if you happen to hear it at the right time, it might strike a chord and make sense to you. The moment when people catch on to or assimilate my teachings will differ depending on the person. Even a topic that has been read about many times can be understood at different levels based on your state of mind when it is read, or it can sometimes have no effect on you at all. I want to state this at the beginning of my talk.

The story of a kitten trying to "catch" happiness

The mindset of seeking prosperity is similar to the attitude of pursuing happiness. In the past, I used the story of a kitten to explain the nature of happiness, and wrote about it in the opening message ("A Guide for the Mind") in *Happy Science Monthly Magazine*. Here is the story:

A little kitten learned that happiness for a cat was in its tail, so it began chasing after its own tail trying hard to catch happiness. Yet no matter how hard the kitten chased after its tail, it could not catch it. The kitten just went round and round in circles. Looking at the kitten's situation, an old cat explained, "If you just do what you should do, your tail will naturally follow after you."

This is an allegory I found in a book by an American psychologist. Among the stories I read in my youth, this one left a great impression on me.

Strangely enough, happiness will remain out of reach if you chase after it, but if you naturally keep moving forward without paying attention to it, it will follow after you. Happiness is something you already own; it belongs to you, like a tail on a cat. As long as you walk your own way naturally and diligently, it will always follow you. If, on the other hand, you chase it believing that happiness is somewhere beyond your grasp, it will escape you. You will eventually become exhausted like the kitten that gets dizzy after going round and round, and give up, thinking how hard it is to capture happiness.

Essentially, happiness exists within you. It is part of you and you already have it. Yet if you try to grab it, you cannot. If, instead, you do not think about trying to get it and simply lead a decent life—study, work, act, think, and do things that must be done as a matter of course, then happiness will follow you without your noticing. This is the nature of happiness. Those who have lived 40, 50 or 60 years or more will probably agree with this; they may even be reminded of their experiences that prove it to be true.

Especially when people are young, they try their best to chase after the "tail of happiness" and sometimes feel anguish because they cannot catch it, no matter what they do. They may think they almost have it, but the moment they try to grab it, it moves away. "Wait! That tail!" they may say and keep chasing it, only to find themselves unable to catch up. Eventually, they will experience a change of heart, and tell themselves, "That's enough. I thought I could be happy by catching the tail, but I don't care anymore. I will just do what I should do every day." If they go about their own business in this way, they will come to understand that they can move their tail any way they want. This way of thinking can be applied in every situation.

Prosperity does not exist somewhere far from you

This chapter's theme, prosperity, is one way in which happiness blooms. In essence, prosperity goes beyond personal fulfillment and encompasses larger entities such as families, companies or even nations; the grand scale of national prosperity could also be included in this discussion. Prosperity has many levels of magnitude, but regardless of the level, the story earlier can be applied to it.

Prosperity is, like happiness, an element that exists within you; it will follow you if you are determined to move forward. However, many people are unaware of it and seek it somewhere over the mountains, or somewhere far and beyond. They might be like Utopian socialists. The word "Utopia" originated from the meaning of "no place" or "nowhere," and Utopian socialism is an idea that utopia is somewhere, and once we get there, we can possess that which is not currently in existence.

In *The Laws of Success* (New York: IRH Press, 2017), I included a story about a town of successful people, and pointed out that one must first achieve success in order to live there. Those who have yet to succeed would naturally want to join the town of successful people, believing they could become rich if they were able to live there. But in reality, wearing ragged clothes with no job or money, they would not be accepted as residents.

To the fortuneless traveler the mayor would say, "You must have passed a village along the way before you arrived here. There, you should have first learned some trade or developed some knowledge, earned some money and made yourself presentable. There are such steps you need to take. Only after completing these steps before coming here will you then be welcomed as our friend and enjoy the fruits of success with us. Why have you skipped over all these steps and come here unprepared?

"No one would want to invite someone like you who dresses like a poverty-stricken beggar into their home. We wouldn't want to keep company with someone like a beggar wandering around obviously expecting a handout. If, instead, you were dressed in a neat suit and tie like a successful businessman, residents would be curious about what business opportunities they could hear from you and would want to listen to what you had to say. Otherwise, you would only cause us unease. There is a process you have to go through. You cannot just try to grab good results by skipping this process." This story is another way of teaching the same lesson.

Prosperity is often compared to the growth of a plant: A planted seed will sprout, grow stems, put out leaves, develop buds and eventually come into full bloom. Along the same lines, there is a period in life when a person reaches full bloom. For a company or organization, this would be the time when it experiences a major success and everyone involved feels happy to have made some progress, sensing that the current year is much better than the last, and that next year will be even better. When employees from that company go home, they tell their spouses how well things are going, and the spouses also feel happy, making comments like, "It seems like things are going well for you at work. Your company seems to be doing great." When people are experiencing these positive feelings, we can say they are enjoying prosperity.

So how can we experience this? It is not by going someplace special to find Utopia or meeting a special person who gives you some magical tool to make money.

Of course, there certainly are such stories. For example, there is the Japanese folktale about a boy who plays with an ogre and is given a magical wooden hammer. Another story tells of a man who goes deep into the mountains and finds Yoro Falls, which flows with sake (rice liquor). When he takes the sake to his sick old father to drink, his father's illness is cured. However, these are merely stories and simply do not happen in reality. If applied to real life, it would be like experiencing unexpected success by chance. Of course, great things like this can occur by chance during one's lifetime, but they are not things many people should aim for.

2

The Cycle of Success to Achieve Prosperity

Lessons from a movie about how to use money

In October 2018, the Happy Science movie, *The Laws of the Universe – Part I* (Executive Producer and original story by Ryuho Okawa) premiered in theaters. A week later, another movie, *Oku-Otoko* (*"Million Dollar Man"*) by director Keishi Otomo was released. The two films competed for box-office rankings, and apparently our movie ended up doing better than *Million Dollar Man*. I went to see the movie on a weekday around the end of its run. As expected, the plot centered on the theme, "What if you unexpectedly won ¥300 million (about US$3 million)?"

The main character, who wins the lottery, looks on the Internet to search what has become of past lottery winners, and discovers that in many cases they end up miserable. He then goes to a bank, where he is given many reasons why he should deposit the money there, such as, "Having millions at hand is like a curse," "It's better not to keep it in cash," or "Let us help you manage your funds." He decides to go and see one of his college classmates who launched an IT-related business venture and successfully made a fortune, to ask his advice on what to do with the money.

According to the book the movie is based on, the friend made more than ¥15 billion (about US$150 million) through his own business. The two characters became friends through the Rakugo (traditional Japanese comic storytelling) Club during college, and have not seen each other in over a decade since graduation. The main character goes to see him expecting that someone who made such a fortune will know how to use money.

His friend tells him to withdraw all the money, saying, "You say you have money in the bank, but it won't feel real unless you actually see it for yourself. Withdraw all the money you have in the bank." He does what his friend says.

The friend also tells him, "You can only get the feel of how much money you have by spending it. First, you've got to appreciate the value of money." They throw an extravagant party at the friend's luxury high-rise apartment complex, inviting hostesses from nightclubs, hiring sushi chefs to make fresh sushi upon request and bartenders to mix drinks for the guests.

The main character falls asleep after partying hard. When he wakes up the next morning, he finds himself alone in the messy apartment. Fearing for the security of his money, he goes to check the safe in the room where he kept it. The money is gone and so is his friend. He is shocked, for he trusted his close friend. Discovering he was deceived, he sets out in search of his friend.

The movie depicts the struggles the main character goes through to retrieve his money. I will not give away more details, but that is the basic story line. The movie concludes with the moral: there are things money cannot buy, such as trust or friendship. Certainly, some people may regard money in that way.

Hardly anyone will teach you how to use money

To begin with, money is hard to earn. It is already difficult to develop the habit of making and saving it. Money will not come in unless you are successful. Many people may think that it is already very tough to earn and save money before even getting the chance to use it. Yet in reality, once you have earned money, there is hardly anyone who will teach you how to use it.

I have never met anyone who taught me how to use money. There are many books on how to make money, but hardly anyone has written about how to use it. There are certainly people who spend plenty of money, but writing and publishing a book about how they spend it would be like showing off. If you made public how much money you have, people would soon flock to you to take advantage of it. Tax collectors would also come around to check to make sure you have not committed fraud. Naturally, the richer people are, the less likely they are going to reveal their spending habits. In reality, they will not tell you how they spend their money and want to keep it a secret.

Now that I have managed Happy Science for more than 30 years, the amount of cash flow has grown quite large. When I was still a salaried employee at a company, although saving a certain amount of money was one of the goals I set for myself, I had no idea how to use it. When I actually started Happy Science, I had to consider how to make good use of the money that had accumulated. Since no one had taught me, I had to make decisions on my own and later examine whether those choices were the right ones. I went through this experience again and again.

After that, it is all about intuition. Whether or not one's intuition is right depends on how one has lived up until then as a human being. Although you may win ¥300 million or US$3 million, if you use it to gamble on horse or bicycle races, or gaming in Las Vegas, the money will soon be gone.

The difficulty of creating a cycle of success: Fundraising, investing, and making a profit

After I saw *Million Dollar Man*, I asked one of my secretaries who came with me to see it, "What would you do if you got ¥300 million?" The secretary pondered a little and said, "Maybe I would make a film." I replied that a movie with only a ¥300-million budget would not be very big, far from the scale of the films Happy Science has produced. On hearing this, the secretary was very surprised.

Indeed, making a movie is one way of using money. Some people will waste money by making one that fails to capture people's hearts, while others are successful, which allows them to create another film. Yet others can amplify their investment to a greater extent, using tens of millions of yen to make a movie and earning billions of yen from it. But such cases are quite rare. In most circumstances, it is difficult just to break even.

The main part of a movie producer's job is to obtain funding from sponsors. This task is harder than the actual filming. Most Japanese movies do not have executive producers. It is uncommon to have someone with this title. Happy Science movies always have one; the series of a live-action film, *Rurouni Kenshin* (*"Samurai X"*), also had a foreign sponsor. Executive producers are almost synonymous with being sponsors who put up the money. Some may have a degree of influence over the movie's content and demand, for example, to have a Hollywood-style film. Nevertheless, in most situations, people simply regard the executive producer as a funding source; the same is probably true for me. I do not mind being regarded as a sponsor, but I still offer my opinions and guidance.

In order to keep producing movies, you need to maintain a certain level of success. Otherwise, it is difficult to continue. If movie projects fail repeatedly, the whole production company will suffer and may crash. From this we can say that a cycle of success needs to be created to achieve prosperity.

Suppose you invest ¥300 million or US$3 million to make a movie. If it makes a profit from box-office sales, then it will give you the courage to make another one. If it earns a very large profit, it could cover the cost of producing the next movie.

Unfortunately, though, it is very unlikely for Japanese films to attain that level. Making a movie that breaks even is already considered satisfactory. In reality, most movies end up in the red financially, even those that cost just tens of millions of yen. It is difficult to entice audiences into theaters, because not many Japanese people watch movies in theaters. This is a harsh reality.

The way you use your money reflects your true character

So first, you must earn and accumulate some amount of money. Next, it is essential to know how to use it—where to invest it, or what one finds necessary to spend it on. This kind of decision-making clearly reveals each person's true character.

Take, for example, the purchase of a house. During the past period of rapid economic growth in Japan, assets were expected to continue rising. Therefore, it was considered better to buy a house earlier in life and to carry a 25- or 30-year mortgage on the assumption that it would be better to have your own house when your children are still small. Most people at the time held this belief. In contrast, others are cautious about making such a large financial commitment and find it safer to wait until their children grow up and become independent adults. They buy a house only after they retire with their retirement money in order to spend the rest of their lives there. There are thus different ways of thinking, and one's way of thinking will dictate one's future.

3

The Mindset to Invite Prosperity

Your mindset will determine
Whether or not you will be successful

In this chapter, I do not intend to talk only about money. I would like to further describe the mental attitude that is the basis of how to achieve prosperity. The crucial point is your state of mind, or your mental attitude, to succeed, as it is what will invite prosperity. The kind of mental attitude or mindset you have will actually determine whether or not you will be successful. These are true words, but in practice, it is not very easy to change your mindset.

To use the earlier analogies, going into the deepest recesses of unexplored mountains to find Yoro Falls, where sake flows, is almost impossible; so is encountering someone who will hand you a magic mallet that gives you money. As illustrated by the tail of a cat, what brings you happiness or prosperity actually lies within you.

Your mindset, or in other words, your mental attitude, will in fact bring about success and prosperity. There is such a way of thinking.

A commonly accepted formula for success

So, what kind of mental attitude do we need to have? That is precisely what I want to talk about.

Usually people do not know it and tend to think, "You have to attend a cram school from a young age to enter a better school. Once you enter a high-ranking school and receive a diploma, you can secure a good job. After that, your academic records will speak for you and you will be rewarded with success." This is the typical idea of parents who solely focus on academic achievement, and the basic sales pitch of cram schools to bait their customers with dreams. I suppose that is one way.

What would have become, however, of those who attended a cram school from elementary school onward, who entered prestigious middle and high schools through examinations, who used different study methods from those in normal public schools, who studied extra through yet another cram school or private tutors, and finally entered a first-rate university? Objectively speaking, after all that effort to get into a first-rate university through lots of studying, using cram schools, and attending prestigious middle and high schools, if they chose to advance to a secure, big-name company, their ultimate annual income would most likely fall within the range of ¥8-12 million (about US$80-120 thousand) in Japan.

Even if you have pushed yourself hard for a long period of 10 to 20 years while receiving encouragement from those around you, you can only hope to reach the position of department manager, while others remain section chiefs. Depending on the company's size, you might become a managing director, but that is the best you can hope for. Even with a special license or certification, the annual income level would be ¥12-20 million (about US$120-200 thousand).

Doctors are said to earn a little more, but those with private practices have higher operating costs, so they apparently need an annual income of more than ¥40 million (about US$400 thousand) to run their business. Some clinics are in the red, so they have to seek out a bank loan or financial aid from family members to make ends meet. That is the usual case.

Hired doctors receive less pay, at a little higher than the average-salaried company employees. They must leave the hospital upon reaching retirement age, as do salaried employees, so they cannot expect to earn large amounts of money.

Recently in Japan, some medical schools were accused of tampering with applicants' entrance exam scores, but it is uncertain whether studying for another four or five years after graduation before finally getting admitted into medical school will pay off in the end. You may believe you have followed a guaranteed formula for success, but the success you gain with that formula might not be as great as expected. At best, you can secure a job in a highly-regarded company and can earn a stable living, perhaps affording you an above average life. To put it another way, it will only allow you to afford sending your children to cram schools and getting admitted to prestigious private schools, and eventually to top-level universities, just as your parents did for you. Many people end up putting themselves in that kind of "success" cycle.

Can you take a step Beyond the normal path of success?

Even among those who have taken such a route, some will feel their expectations have been somewhat unmet after entering university. Up until then, they have worked hard to enter a top-tier university, believing that studying hard would lead them to great success. However, after encountering many similar students, they realize they are not so special and suddenly lose their self-respect and drive. There are many such people. Or, they experience this shock after graduating from university. Even if they may have been able to persevere through college, they suddenly lose motivation when they start working at a company. Again, there are many such people.

In society, certain jobs offer dreams, such as entertainers, professional athletes, professional shogi (Japanese chess) players, novelists, and artists. Those who make it big appear to have brilliant, attractive lives. Some novelists become popular and make a fortune, but such people are quite rare. The probability of becoming a popular author is definitely much less than that of being a successful salaried employee.

Becoming an artist that can sell paintings with million-dollar price tags would require luck so extreme that it would be like surviving all nuclear bombs exploding everywhere without suffering harm. Competition is fierce in the entertainment business as well. Many are forced to work for low pay, and sometimes must do any job given to them, including ones they loathe. People tend to only see the bright side, but competition is very fierce in any field, and many people fail.

Therefore, it is a big mistake to set your final destination at the level that average people generally consider a "success." Whether you can take an extra step forward will, in fact, be the crossroad of your life.

What does it take to advance one step forward? That is the aforementioned mental attitude, or mindset. There is a time when you have to focus your energy to learn from failures in life and turn them into positive experiences. In study or work, when you start out something new, you will actually experience a lot of failures. It is such times when you can see a big difference between those who have received life lessons and mastered how to live through difficult times, and those who have not.

Unfortunately, those who study reluctantly simply to look good on paper will not do as well as expected, even if they graduate from a good university. It is a big mistake to see a good educational background as a kind of decoration that will guarantee you a stable life. Japanese society no longer works that way, not since the 1990s.

Prosperity is a chain of success and its expansion

Prosperity is, after all, a series of consecutive successes. It is also to spread your success to others. You need to spread it to the people who work for you, to your family, and to the company you work for. This is a form of prosperity, and how you create such a mindset is truly important.

It is possible to have high levels of motivation for a certain period of time. You will be happy when you are feeling good, but things do not go well all the time. Take, for example, a sports day at school. Not every game can be won; you win some games and lose others. In marathon races, too, you win some races while you lose others. The same is true in life. Anyone will feel great and do well when they are on the track to success, but unexpected accidents can happen, such as injuries, illness, setbacks, or disappointment. That is the key moment. How will you put yourself back on the track to success? This is the most crucial point.

4

How to Practice the Mindset
To Achieve Prosperity

Practice 1: Always consider your "batting average"

Here, I would like to share a few main points I learned and practiced as a young man. I have also spoken about them from different angles on various occasions.

One is, as Dale Carnegie often mentioned, to always consider your "batting average." Baseball players all experience a period when they slump. Throughout the season, there are times when they hit well and when they cannot. Yet they can get through the rough spots if they are confident of their ability to produce results to maintain their average by the end of the season. They can continue their training steadily while taking a rest when necessary. Then, they will eventually recover. Those who are unsure of their batting average will sometimes find themselves in deeper holes after experiencing a slump, whereas those who are confident of hitting .300 can be sure that they will revert to the normal batting average within the year.

The same holds true for work. Even if you experience a failure, you can tell yourself, "My past records show that I am successful

70-80 percent of the time, so I'm sure I can make up for it." If you persevere with such thinking, you can overcome a loss.

Thus, consider your "batting average." This is one of the lessons I have always kept in mind.

Practice 2: Remember that no one ever kicks a dead dog

Up until now, I have composed a lot of music and written many lyrics. This usually requires a sensitive disposition. When I was young, I used to write poetry as well. As a young man, I may have appeared bold and strong to others because I freely spoke what was on my mind, but in truth I was rather sensitive. When others would retort, thinking I wouldn't be affected by any negative remarks, their words were piercing and hurt me quite a bit. I often had such experiences.

There may be times when you feel that your pride has been hurt or your honor defamed. However, how many days you spend in anguish or how many years you prolong your agony is up to you. You can grieve over a past experience for decades, or you can get over it in a day. It is completely within your control. At such times, you must be determined to get stronger and overcome it yourself.

One of the phrases that saved me from such struggles was another phrase by Dale Carnegie, "Remember that no one ever kicks a dead dog." Another similar expression goes, "No one beats a dog drowning in water." If a dog barks wildly, some people may feel like kicking it, but hardly anyone would kick a lifeless dog lying by the roadside, or beat a drowning dog in a river.

The same holds true for people. If people try to "kick" you, it means you are "barking" a lot, because they feel threatened and are afraid you might bite them; so, they defend themselves by attacking you. This means that you are barking aggressively at others. The expression, "No one ever kicks a dead dog" indeed makes a point.

You may have experienced being mocked, humiliated or criticized in various ways, but that is precisely because you are attracting the attention of others. You need to know this as an objective fact. People criticize you because you stand out. Maybe they are jealous. Some people will continuously accuse you even though their comments hurt you, but that is because they believe you are not affected by what they say. If you were a "dead dog," they would not attempt to kick you anymore, so their continuous attack means they still regard you as strong and impervious to their criticism.

I myself had this experience when I was in my early 20s; I bore the aggression of people 20 years older at work. They apparently thought, "We must attack him now, because we never know when our positions will become reversed. We will be the target of his hostility when he becomes our superior, so let's bully him while we still can." This was such an absurd idea that I could hardly believe; I felt like asking them why they didn't care more about their own promotions.

Three senior employees of or near section chief status were hostile toward me, an energetic, capable junior worker who had only been employed for three or four years. They got together and acted abusively toward me, as if to say, "You might soon get promoted over us and mistreat us as a manager in the future, so we'll teach you a lesson now."

I was astonished to find out there were people with such a mentality; I had no notion of it. I wanted to say, "You feel threatened by someone over 15 years younger than you, and that's why you try to strike me down. But I won't be a threat to you because by the time I get elevated to an important position, you would most likely be retired. You have nothing to worry about, so why not be less threatening and work harmoniously?"

It was unbelievable but there are people who try hard to cut down a potential threat in advance in such an obvious way. They are actually beating a dog with a stick, believing the dog is still not drowning. They believe they must be aggressive because the dog might bite them. They are trying to make it obedient. I too was once the target of this kind of attack. I wondered what caused them to perceive me in such a way when I was actually a very naive person. I worked hard out of strong loyalty to the company, not out of selfish motivation.

The company I worked for did not pay based on a commission system. The profits derived from each employee were taken in and paid out by the company, so an individual's personal contributions were not remunerated to that person directly. This meant that my hard work would go to benefit others' higher salaries and bonuses as well. This was my thinking, but some people did not share the same view.

Even if you face such a situation, it is important to bounce back. This is the lesson of Carnegie's words, "No one ever kicks a dead dog."

Practice 3:
Don't try to saw sawdust instead learn lessons

Another quote by Dale Carnegie is "Don't try to saw sawdust." Sawdust is the remainder produced after you saw a log. Carnegie said there are many people in the world who try to saw sawdust.

Sawdust can be used as kindling to start a fire, but it is no more than sawdust. Yet, some people try to saw even sawdust. If you look back, you may also find you've done it.

There are people who remember a mistake they made a year ago, five years ago, or even further back, and blame the past mistake for causing them to be in their current situation, even though they cannot do anything about it now. Once in a while, you need to check and see if you are trying to saw sawdust, instead of a log. I too would often do this.

Some people fail at their business and face bankruptcy. Some of them may then find another job and work for someone else, while others may bounce back and start another business. In any case, failure is like sawdust; it cannot be sawed further. While you need to learn from your experiences, it is essential to dispose of the rest as sawdust.

There are people who dwell on their failures too long. Those who constantly complain are mostly this type of person.

Practice 4: Turn life's lemons into lemonade

Another phrase from Dale Carnegie that led me to develop Invincible Thinking was "If you have a lemon, make lemonade." I have continued to ponder the meaning of this phrase since I was young.

In English, the word "lemon" suggests something sour-tasting or substandard. For example, when you refer to a vehicle as a lemon, it means that the vehicle is defective. The term "lemon" in English is not usually used in a positive sense. In Japan, it has a slightly better connotation, but in English when you say lemon, it refers to something bad, sour or useless, a defective car, or a defective product, having the image of being of "no use."

When life gives you lemons, Carnegie said, don't feel sorry over those lemons but instead consider making lemonade out of them. You can at least make lemonade by squeezing the lemons and adding some water and sugar; you can even start a business selling lemonade. In the same way, bitterness in life can be converted to something that brings pleasure or joy. You can also turn it into a business idea.

Being a religious leader for over 30 years, I have experienced a number of such situations. I had many failures in the past and was scolded many times. However, these experiences turned out to be truly "delicious dishes" for me. In fact, I could not be a religious leader without them.

If I succeeded in everything I do, people would only say, "That's great of you, well-done," and they could learn nothing more. The truth is that I still have another 90 percent of stories that I cannot tell others; they are stored in my "inner drawers." I can reveal them little by little on different occasions. For example, there might be stories like, "Although I once said that I had suffered heartbreak three times, I have actually had 30 such experiences and..." If I could reveal my past failures endlessly like magicians pulling out a string of handkerchiefs from their pockets, I would never run out of things to talk about.

In reality, it is painful when you fail. You feel pain when you break up with someone you love, get demoted, get a pay cut, receive a smaller bonus, are spoken badly of, get divorced, or when your child does poorly at school. There can be any number of painful experiences, so you should not just accept life's "lemons" as they were, but turn them into lemonade.

You need to apply Invincible Thinking and devise ways to change the bad to create "a delicious drink." Try to seek out hints for a future business, use them as opportunities for your next challenge, or figure out preventive measures to avoid making the same mistake again. Surely you can view them in a positive light and use them as lessons to benefit yourself.

Furthermore, you can form an abstract viewpoint and universalize these lessons to present a new idea or way of life that can be useful to many people, or to create a new mode of thinking. By doing so, you would quite probably succeed on any path, like I did as a religious leader. Entrepreneurs can become successful by learning from the many failures they experience in running their businesses. Politicians can also improve their skills and succeed after undergoing election losses, receiving harsh criticism and defamatory remarks, or even coming last in an election. Using such pain as their springboard, they can make comparative studies by observing other candidates and gradually gain popularity.

If you have managed to master a way to turn your life's lemons into lemonade, this means you have found Yoro Falls, where sake flows, or have been able to grasp a lucky mallet that produces gold coins every time you swing it. There is no need to wait to win the lottery. There is a mountain of treasure waiting for you.

5
Try to Find the Nearby Seeds of Prosperity

Nothing you experience in life is a waste. When you succeed, you can use that experience as a steppingstone for the next success. Use it as secure footing, and you can gain even greater success. When you fail, you can use that failure wisely; you can enrich your heart by increasing the "folds" in your mind to expand your sphere of understanding. You can also broaden your range of topics for conversation, improve your relationships, and your skills of negotiation. Thus, you can evolve and develop in different ways. All these factors will lead you to a successful life.

Therefore, the way to become a million-dollar man is definitely not by winning the lottery. Rather, it is *how* you live your life. Even if a person attends a cram school, an elite high school, and then a top university like the University of Tokyo or Kyoto, Waseda or Keio University, that person will generally end up securing a management position and earning an annual salary of ¥8-12 million (about US$80-120 thousand). That would be decent. A portion of people might not make it and drop out of the rat race, but most of them will achieve such success at best. If you want to achieve greater success, however, you need to change your mindset.

What is this mindset? You must understand that prosperity does not lie somewhere over the mountains, far and beyond, or in the deepest recesses of mountains that no one has ever explored. Rather, the seed of prosperity is to be found within you, or around you—in your family, or in the very job you are now doing. It is essential to be aware of this.

Please adopt the habit of looking for the seeds of prosperity in what you have and shape your thinking in this way. Then, everything will turn into an opportunity. I hope you change your way of thinking in this manner.

In this chapter I talked theoretically about how to think so as to invite prosperity. I hope you will contemplate it deeply and put it into practice.

THOUGHTS WILL GENERATE EXTREMELY STRONG POWER

Whether the future is positive or negative,

Whether it is optimistic or pessimistic,

Whether it is happy or unhappy,

Depends on the seeds in your mind.

If you want to make your future a happy one,

You must plant positive seeds in your mind

And cultivate them.

And in order to cultivate these seeds,

You must constantly deepen your thoughts

In a repeated process.

When you feel you are beaten down

By pessimistic thoughts,

You have to self-generate positive ones

That are strong enough to repel them.

This means you must gather your will and make an effort.

Do what you can do today

And think about your hopes for tomorrow.

If you are about to come under

A negative way of thinking,

It is essential to produce and radiate

A positive way of thinking to fight against it.

Human beings cannot have

Two contradicting thoughts at once.

A happy person cannot feel unhappy,

And an unhappy person cannot feel happy.

It is impossible to talk of sad things as you laugh

Or to talk of happy things as you cry with a sad face.

Humans can only think of one thing at a time.

Thus, what occupies your mind

Is extremely important.

Have a positive image of yourself,

Always hold a clear picture of yourself

Developing more, succeeding more,

Contributing to the world more,

Becoming happier,

Thereby making people around you happier, too.

When you feel like you are losing ground

To negative thoughts,

Summon your courage

And put out positive ones once again.

If you can do so in this world,

Then you can do it in another world as well.

That is the victory of life.

In order to reverse your fate,

It is very important to form the right mindset

And the right way of thinking.

I hope you will learn that

Thoughts will generate extremely strong power.

Chapter TWO

THE LAW OF
CAUSE AND
EFFECT

There is No Success Without Proportionate Effort

Lecture given on November 14, 2018
at Happy Science General Headquarters, Tokyo, Japan

1

Three Thousand Lectures
In Thirty-plus Years

✧   ✧   ✧

My first lecture that launched
The Happy Science movement

On November 23, 1986, I gave my first lecture at the Happy Science Launch Commemoration Session; it was the First Turning of the Wheel of Truth at Happy Science. Looking back on that day, I remember there were 87 people gathered from all around the country to listen to my lecture. No more than 100 people heard me speak at the start of the Happy Science movement. This thought fills me with deep emotion.

It is a little embarrassing to say this, but before the start of my lecture, I was considering hiding myself away from the world for a while if I failed, even though I had already renounced the world to be a religious leader. I gave this talk in front of an audience of about 90 people that I didn't know. They came from different parts of the country, including Hokkaido and Kyushu, and most of them were older than me. Since it was my first time giving a lecture in such a setting, I really had no idea if it would be successful.

As a matter of fact, my public speaking skills were still lacking, and I tended to speak too fast because I was nervous. I gave the talk, followed by a question-and-answer session, which took about 2 hours and 40 minutes, but I spoke so fast that the content of my lecture would have been more than enough to fill one of my books. I was indeed nervous. I feared that my performance was so poor and unpolished that my lecture on the First Turning of the Wheel of Truth was never made into a CD or DVD for public use. I would rather die from shame than relive those moments by watching or listening to my inexperienced lecture.

In my hometown, my mother viewed the video recording and said she could not bear watching it. She could feel how nervous I was and said that her heart ached to watch it. I'm sure it did. I suppose she could feel my tension.

Still, despite these negative points, the attendees who afforded to travel that day to attend my lecture probably felt there was a more positive side to it; the light of Truth was ignited in their hearts and spread nationwide.

Assisting spirits advised me not to think of anything When standing at the podium

Looking back at that time, if I had been told the details of the work I would be doing, the kind of work I am doing now, I am not sure I would have believed it. I would have only thought, "It might be a possibility one day in the distant future."

I now comfortably give public lectures on occasions such as the Celebration of the Lord's Descent or the El Cantare Celebration at huge venues like Makuhari Messe or the Saitama Super Arena. However, if I had suggested, "The First Turning of the Wheel of Truth should not be held in the rather small Nippori Shuhan Kaikan, which is 60-70m² (about 700ft²) and can be rented for free. Let's use a bigger venue like Makuhari Messe or the Saitama Super Arena instead," then I can easily imagine this would have led to a major failure.

Higher spirits have been supporting Happy Science since those times, and the 30-plus years that have passed until now have not only changed me, but also affected the awareness and enlightenment of these assisting spirits.

In December 2018, I gave a lecture at Makuhari Messe titled, "The Power to Make Miracles" (see Chapter 6). This title was given to me by our General Headquarters. To reveal a backstage secret, although the lecture titles are usually planned ahead of time, I have never prepared the content of my talks beforehand. This has been true from my very first lecture and all lectures since then.

Normally, you would want to take notes or write an outline for a lecture. At first, I too wanted to do it a week or a day before, or even on the day of the lecture. Since those times, I have usually decided beforehand which higher spirit among many Happy Science assisting spirits would support my lecture that day. In the early days, I would ask the assisting spirits, "What should I talk about in the lecture?" The answer would always be: "Do not think of anything." They would say, "Empty your mind and just stand at the podium." This has always been the case. They never allowed me to think; "Just stand at the podium" was all they would say.

I was told something like, "Stand at the podium, and words will naturally come out. Unless you believe in this simple truth, you cannot be a great man of religion." That is how it has been from the beginning.

Reporters from the mass media might imagine that I write speeches and practice delivering them many times before I give an hour-long talk in public. I do make mistakes during a lecture, but only rarely; since the early days, I have spoken almost without flaws, even at large-scale lectures. In general, this is probably impossible, even for newscasters, so they probably assume that I always practice 10-15 times before my talk.

The truth is that I simply stand at the podium without preparing any thoughts; I merely have the lecture's title. This is true even now. If you were to ask me, for example, "Do you get nervous when you give a lecture at Makuhari Messe?" my answer would be, "Sure, sometimes. But only for 5-10 seconds."

I do not feel nervous when I am in the dressing room. When I stand in the stage wings and see the serious-looking Chief

Secretary of Religious Affairs Headquarters with headphones, signaling with his hand to start the count down, "5, 4, 3, 2, 1," I think to myself, "Oh, it's time to start." As I walk toward the podium, looking around at the audience clapping their hands, I think to myself, "Ah, today is the day." At the podium, I face my audience and begin talking. I have given lectures in this manner for over 30 years. It may sound strange, but on this matter, I have strong confidence in myself.

I have been preparing daily for over 30 years To give a talk on any subject

I have confidence that help from the heavenly world will come to me at the time of the lecture, but there is one step necessary before reaching that level. With the spirit of self-help, I have continuously made preparations daily for more than 30 years, so I am able to give lectures on any topic. That is the truth. It should not be said that I neglect to prepare for lectures; the fact is that I am prepared to speak about any topic.

I am certainly capable of speaking on any title given to me, for I have continued to make efforts accordingly. There is no doubt that I have gained competence through accumulated efforts.

Recently, I was driven past Hibiya Public Hall in Tokyo. It reminded me of the time I gave a lecture there to an audience of about 2,000 people. I remember previously feeling that giving a lecture in a place like Hibiya Public Hall with a capacity of 2,000 seats would rate me as a top-class lecturer. Two thousand people is about the highest limit in audience size for the average lecturer. Even for the leader of Japan's Liberal Democratic Party, speaking at Hibiya Public Hall for party conventions would be at his maximum limit.

In my case, thankfully, many people come from around the country; my talks are also broadcast via satellite. Furthermore, my lectures are printed and published. Books made from lectures held 10, 20, or 30 years ago are still available for people to read. I am truly grateful for this.

The importance and joy of achieving steady growth

After all this, though, I am glad that I have not been so easily satisfied with myself. I have often spoken on this from different angles, but unfortunately, there are more people who do not understand my point than those who do.

I feel sad when I see young people born much later than me to be quick to think of themselves as well-accomplished. I wonder why they are so easily satisfied with themselves. In a way, they appear to be applauding themselves, boasting about how great they are. The expectations they demand of themselves may be very low, or they might lack confidence so badly that they need constant self-praise. Or, they receive so many bad comments every day that they need to fight back with self-compliments. Whatever the reason, I often find that people are too easily contented with a low level of achievement, or too easily satisfied with what they have done. Of course, I know that not everyone is like that.

Some young staff members who were born around the time of the First Turning of the Wheel of Truth now hold executive positions at Happy Science. This makes me think that people grow very quickly. However, I hope that people will understand and savor the importance and joy of steady growth, just as trees grow annual rings with each passing year.

When I was young, I did not have much confidence; I felt ashamed or discouraged by my failures and was often disappointed with myself. However, looking back on those days, I now feel I should praise myself a little for not having become too proud of myself so easily.

At any stage of my life, I have never thought that my work was complete. It is the same even now. If, for example, I had been satisfied with book sales of 10 thousand copies, it would not have gone any further than that. I continue to publish books because I regrettably still feel that my teachings have yet to spread around the world. I gave my 2,830th or so lecture, which this chapter is based on, because not everyone has heard my teachings. This is my endless fight. Still, I am sure I am making progress little by little, like the growth rings of trees.

I first accumulated about 2,800 lectures, and then 2,900. Confidence grows in me bit by bit after each talk. Since I have given so many lectures, I have experienced a variety of circumstances; large and small audiences, small towns and big cities, or domestic locations and overseas venues. I have also witnessed the unique conditions of each country and city I have visited. These experiences have helped me to cultivate and build mental resilience. I can recall every particular situation, as well as the way I handled it and pushed through to complete my mission. I believe these experiences slowly worked to develop my resilience, which has served me for self-protection.

My speaking at a large-scale venue may appear to be effortless work, but it is certainly due to my effort to maintain an environment where I am constantly in tune with the heavenly world, and more importantly, it is due to my continuous efforts to remain prepared all the time.

It is also true that, every year I push the frontier of my work a little bit farther away, and gradually take on work that I have never tried before. When entering a new frontier, my accumulated effort gives me confidence, supporting and safeguarding me. That is why I am able to ask myself, "Is it really time for me to take on a new challenge?" and then make a decision on it.

That is what happened for example, when I started overseas missionary work, and when we built our own schools and a university. Making movies and composing music also began this way. More recently, I have given out information regarding "space people." This, too, was possible thanks to the confidence I have built for more than 30 years. Even if I were criticized for what I recently revealed, I would not be crushed so easily whatever the criticism. I would even feel like saying, "Go ahead and try to refute every detail of what I say, if you can." Thus, the more achievements pile up, the more courage develops, helping me to take on new challenges. In this sense, making continuous effort is very important.

2
Nothing Can Be Achieved in a Single Leap

✧ ✧ ✧

Shakyamuni Buddha's effort

This chapter's theme, "the Law of Cause and Effect," is a topic I have already spoken about many times. This simple truth seems rather difficult for people to understand. Most people soon forget about it, although they might understand it when they hear about it.

Put simply, this law says, "Without a cause, there is no effect." If you don't sow seeds, there will be no grain to harvest; if you don't plant seeds, there will be no fruit to eat. Certainly, other factors such as fertilizer, water, and sunshine are necessary to grow plants, but the whole process always follows the Law of Cause and Effect.

For example, Gautama Siddhartha attained Great Enlightenment and became Buddha, but this was not because he was born the prince of Kapilavastu. Compared to general citizens, being born a prince may have allowed him to receive a good education and develop a higher awareness in the early stages of his life, but he abandoned everything and left home at the age of 29. He then undertook ascetic training for six years, eventually attaining enlightenment, and taught about it to his first five disciples. That was the start of Buddhism.

Even though he was born a prince, he abandoned everything to start from zero, and engaged in spiritual discipline on his own. He once trained under those referred to as gurus for a few months, but finding the training unsatisfactory, he left them and pursued his own path. He then attained enlightenment and set out to tell people of what he discovered. In doing so, he deepened his awareness, and thus accumulated enlightenment after enlightenment.

As his religious order expanded with various types of people joining, new teachings became necessary because the new members had different backgrounds and required other suitable teachings. In addition, as problems arose more frequently in regard to the organization's operations, new precepts and rules were set accordingly. In this way, Shakyamuni Buddha made efforts to overcome each new challenge he faced. I believe that the accumulation of these efforts resulted in a large religious community, and served as power for it to endure for future generations.

Surely Gautama Siddhartha did not attain enlightenment in a single leap; being born at the Palace of Kapilavastu did not make him Buddha. Even if he had been born in other circumstances and had taken a different route, he would have followed a similar process to eventually become Buddha.

The hero's journey seen In both Eastern and Western cultures

In religious circles, people born of noble status can sometimes experience unexpected difficulties. For example, in the long-lasting but now rather waning Tibetan Buddhism, the Dalai Lama is chosen at birth. The Japanese Imperial Family also has an unbroken familial line inherited by birth. Those of noble birth or born from noble seed can sometimes become great people. In reality, however, it is not easy to attain enlightenment or to become virtuous when one is born into these circumstances. It is true that the outcome depends on the potential of one's soul, and some souls reach their full potential and achieve greatness. But it is worthy to note that the Monomyth, or Hero's Journey, is held in both Eastern and Western cultures.

There is a common tale that someone of noble birth leaves his palace or city, away from his familiar environment, and experiences various ordeals in unknown places. After overcoming these difficulties, he returns home and finds his true form with a new awakening, finally becoming a noble king or prince, or an enlightened one. This is a typical experience that makes someone a hero. Many such stories can be found in Japan and other countries.

The point, of course, is not simply the departure from home; one needs to discipline oneself while being away. Those born into noble status must confront diverse tribulations and broaden their experience, observe the lives of ordinary people, and learn about their suffering. These will help them to learn and understand many things, which will serve as important elements to make them, for example, a good king, emperor, or Pope.

If, on the other hand, they only grow up to sit on the throne without ever witnessing the lives and suffering of the poor and other ordinary people, they cannot understand these things. Many obstacles block their view, and observing the land afar from a castle tower through a telescope does not allow them to get an idea of people's lives and feelings. It is often said that you should go through adversities when you are young, even if you have to pay for them. Considering the outcome, I totally agree with this, although some might claim that my mentioning such things means I am starting to get old.

When you are young, it is natural to feel that trials and tribulations are unpleasant experiences you would rather avoid. After some decades, however, you will feel more often that each of these served as a seed for you to grow into who you are, though you may not have realized this in the past.

You can improve yourself at any age,
Following the Law of Cause and Effect

When I talk about the mind, young people tend to think that the mind or heart is synonymous with emotions. Many of them only understand the mind to be the basic feelings of joy, anger, sorrow and pleasure. Emotions will naturally develop in a baby as it grows up, but you need to go through various experiences to discover the mind, which will help you to form many folds of understanding in your mind. As you develop many folds in your mind, you will be able to teach the Truth in ways that suit different people.

There are people who remain unable to understand the mind. They only understand their minds, but not those of others. There are also many people who do not even recognize their own minds. They are deceived by their minds, becoming deluded by their careers, family status, or the companies they work for; they are unable to make their minds transparent to see themselves honestly.

Therefore, we need to go back to the starting point, to the Law of Cause and Effect, and always remind ourselves, "No cause, no effect." This is true in one's youth, early adulthood, prime, and twilight years. You cannot necessarily say, for example, that you are intelligent or physically strong simply because you are young. There are also people who begin to study in middle age and get smarter, or make efforts to become physically stronger. Some might be stronger even in their twilight years.

I know an elderly gentleman, one of my relatives, in his 90s. At his age, he still walks more than 10,000 steps every day. He tries hard to stay fit so as not to have his driver's license taken away. He is indeed incredible. He most likely trained his mind and body when he was young and has kept it up. Even in his 90s, he takes precautions not to lose his driver's license and makes an effort to walk 10,000 paces daily so that those around him will not worry that he is too old to drive.

Not all young people are able to walk that much. A distance of 10,000 steps is about 6 km (about 4 miles), which is not that easy. When I was in preschool, we walked 4 km to and from a site for a field trip. I remember my feet hurting and getting a high fever that evening, which showed that it was very far for a young child. Hiking would also be tough.

Fermenting knowledge to elevate it to wisdom

You cannot achieve anything in a single leap; you need training to acquire a particular skill. Some skills can be lost easily and quickly, while others can be retained for life.

Take, for example, riding a bicycle. Children need training wheels when they begin to ride a bike, but eventually, the wheels are removed, and a parent or other adult will push from behind to help them ride. They practice riding in this way in wide spaces until they can manage to balance on their own. Once you learn to ride a bicycle, you can do so even after an absence of 20 or 30 years. The same is true for swimming. At first, you may be afraid of deep water, but once you learn to swim, the ability sticks, even after a long time. Some skills are not easily lost once you acquire them.

I have just talked about walking, but for four-legged animals, standing on two legs would be extremely difficult. You can see many kinds of four-legged animals in zoos, and many of them have greater physical abilities than humans, being sturdier, with stronger muscles and quicker reflexes. Nevertheless, only a limited number can stand on two legs. Monkeys can. Horses can rear up, lifting their front legs, but cannot walk only on their hind legs. Lions, tigers, and leopards are the same. In the world of animation, animals can sing and dance, but this is hard to believe in real life. Walking on two legs is not easy for them.

In this life, there are many skills you can learn and acquire through experience, and once you master a skill, it becomes yours.

I have spoken about wisdom on many occasions. It is difficult to transform learned knowledge into wisdom. Information is like raw material and is not wisdom; you need to let it rest and ferment, the same way sake is made through fermentation. As you apply your knowledge to real experiences, using it in various situations, it will start to shine and sublimate into wisdom. It is important to have such a view of the world.

Being praised for your intelligence when you are young is a good thing because it means you have made serious efforts at an early age. However, being intelligent at 18 or 19 does not necessarily guarantee your intelligence at 30. It does not mean you are still intelligent at age 40, nor does it determine whether you remain smart or become senile in your 50s or 60s. This depends on your diligent efforts after your school years.

If you continuously make efforts, even a small amount can unexpectedly take you far. To write 100 books might seem challenging, but if you keep writing one book at a time, eventually, you can reach 100. In that process, it is essential that you study, experience various things, and receive inspiration to deepen your thoughts on what you are going to write.

The shallow understanding of those Who quickly believe they are enlightened

The Law of Cause and Effect is indeed important. Some people in their twilight years, for instance, continue their efforts to keep their bodies active even while in wheelchairs, or study something to avoid mental decline. There is a difference between those who make such efforts and those who don't. This is worthy to note.

Some people might think they can attain enlightenment in a single leap through some spiritual experience. Many Japanese religious groups, in particular, seem to hold this type of thinking. Certainly, there is a moment when a significant leap can occur, and it is true that a distinctive difference can be made after the attainment of enlightenment. However, this does not happen without effort.

You cannot reach a 3,000-m (10,000-ft) mountain top in a single bound like Superman. That is naturally impossible. It is only possible if you believe enlightenment is so low that it is merely a step or two above where you are. The crucial point is that you should not quickly feel like you have understood everything and become enlightened after a simple discovery.

Some optimistic people have this tendency. There are many such people among those who practice Zen as well; they suddenly become aware of something and believe they are enlightened. But to me, they are simply intoxicated by the atmosphere. It is just that they were previously unaware of something that ordinary people had already been aware of, and when they become aware of it, they believe they are enlightened. However, their discovery is still shallow.

In the world of enlightenment, you need to advance step by step; you need to make progress in many different fields in order to gain deeper enlightenment. That is what I believe. Thus, it is best to avoid relying on natural attributes from birth, special methods, backdoor routes, personal connections, or unique embellishments to make yourself look good. These are not roads that take you on a long journey.

3
We Can Learn Many Things
From Others

Example 1:
The gap between subjective and objective truths

It may sound like I know things well, but the truth is that I had to learn very basic things from others when I was younger. For example, about a year after starting work, a manager called me to his desk one day to lecture me. He told me, "You may think you are working hard, but you act as if you were singing in the spotlight; as you sing, the audience might leave. You may be singing all by yourself, with no one to listen to you." I was told something like that. It has been nearly 40 years since then, but I still remember it.

I was surprised by his perception of me. I was not really satisfied with my ability, so I was working hard trying to give it my all. But some people saw this as me trying to show off. In their eyes, it probably appeared as if I were trying hard to make myself look much smarter. I realized that some people might actually have felt offended by how I worked.

In reality, freshmen will often find themselves unable to fit into work properly. I also felt strange that I could not work as well as I wanted to. I could not accomplish much, and did not even know what was usual practice and common sense for my coworkers. I felt like this on many occasions.

Example 2: Making copies

Another example is making copies. I was scolded for the way I copied documents. Some busy executives have their secretaries make copies for them, but otherwise, you must do the job by yourself. When I went to make copies, my superior would find fault with me by saying, "Look here, the edges are uneven," or "This document is stapled oddly. Can't you see?" I would then learn the correct way to avoid making crooked copies.

No one had taught me this before; I would only learn certain skills after being yelled at. I realized how neatly and skillfully secretaries made copies, with the corners aligned straight. When copying a book, they made sure there were no dark shadows in the middle. This made me realize that I could not even make copies in a satisfactory manner.

Example 3:
Dealing with confidential documents

At other times, I saw executives make their own copies. I wondered why they did not ask their secretaries to make copies for them, and commented that maybe they didn't know how to delegate work to other people. My superior was appalled and said, "Are you a fool?" He then explained that senior management would sometimes handle highly sensitive, confidential documents that others should not see. They could not even allow their secretaries to view such documents; that was why they did it themselves. He said, "What if they contained personal data? You never know who might happen to see it, or if some papers might be left behind by accident." I had thought that some executives were doing the same work as me, an employee of low rank, but I learned then that some documents had to be treated differently.

Example 4: Making copies for private purposes

Another time, I was scolded for making copies for my own study concerning my new assignment. I was transferred to a new division after returning to Japan from the New York office, where I mostly worked on foreign exchange activities. My new work involved monetary matters and dealings with financial institutions. Since there were no textbooks for me to study, I would cut out or copy bank-related news and other financial articles from *The Nikkei* newspaper in order to make files for my own study. My superior told me I was wasting copies and should learn the content just by reading. He saw me as impudent, but his comment was indeed right.

Example 5: Cutting out newspapers that went to waste

My father once made a similar comment. As a student, I would cut out many articles from newspapers, underline important parts in red, and keep them in my drawer. Seeing what I did, my father said, "I did the same thing when I was young, but most of it was wasted. You just have to learn it by heart." It was certainly true that I later found most of the articles useless. I learned this as I went through these experiences.

There was a time when I would cut out a series of articles featured in a newspaper, and mount and store them in special filing boxes. In that way I was content with my own studies. However, once the series was completed, the articles were compiled to be sold in a book form. I remember feeling shocked at the time. They were political science articles, so I thought it would be good to save them for my studies, but they were later made into a book. I felt betrayed by the author, thinking, "If that was the plan, they should have announced it from the outset; then I wouldn't have troubled myself by cutting and filing them so much." I had such an experience.

The world is full of things to learn. Even for seemingly unimportant matters, we cannot know the "dos and don'ts" unless we are taught them.

Example 6: Answering the phone

Phone calls need to be answered differently, depending on the nature of the conversation. But I had never considered this issue and had always spoken loudly. I was then admonished when my voice reached the other side of the office. I was told that, for confidential matters, I should muffle my voice by covering the phone with one hand so that no one else would hear it. Since no one had taught me, I didn't know that either.

Example 7: Leaving documents on my desk

There was yet another lesson. Once, at lunch time, I rushed out for my break, leaving some documents on my desk. My superior later called me over and asked me, "Are you leaving all those documents facing up? What if someone looked at them while you were out?"

Certainly, the Financial Department handled many money-related documents, so even if they did not have "confidential" stamped on them, I should have been more careful.

During lunch breaks, many people would come and go in the workplace, including bank officers, salespeople from securities and insurance companies, and our staff members from other departments. I was told to turn my paperwork face down and to place a paperweight on it before leaving my desk so that it would not be easily flipped over. Again, I had to be taught this.

One should learn these things in the first or second year of work, and by the third at the latest. There are hundreds and thousands of such tiny details that we need to know. Talking on the phone, as I mentioned earlier, is one such example. Like a fishmonger yelling, "Fresh catch of the day, right here!" I would answer the phone so loudly that everyone in the office could hear, and I did not realize other people's complaints concerning my loud voice. It would be fine for a fishmonger to yell to attract many shoppers but I was scolded, "You are too loud. Can't you see other people are also working here?" I didn't realize it until I was told.

4
Humility Means
Remaining Open to Learning

You will naturally be humble
If you truly want to develop yourself

There are many things that we can only learn when others tell us, so we should not puff up with pride. I often teach people to be humble; this means being open to learning.

People will be happy to teach you if you remain humble. Some will even kindly warn you of dangers when necessary and will take your hand to lead you in the right direction. This is something to be grateful for. In many cases, things you learn in an informal setting will later become your wisdom, compared to things you learn in an official setting.

As a side note, books by successful businessmen are usually based on their own experiences, but the stories are often modified by their editors. For example, management failures are skillfully altered into remarkable success stories of how they overcame hardships and reached their goal, so as not to let them look like mere failures. We cannot always take their stories at face value.

In any case, when you fail at something, it is very important to practice self-reflection or to accept advice from others. To be able to do that, it is essential not to take too much pride in yourself. You should not become conceited.

I mentioned earlier that if you were born into a noble family, you would need to go away from that environment and face hardships to be able to understand the feelings of ordinary people. But even if you do not go far away, you can gain much information and observe many things right where you are if you put your mind to it. If you are too proud of yourself, however, your pride will blind you, leading you to believe that you are different from others. You will then focus merely on benefiting yourself or gaining authority over others. This can be dangerous.

There are certainly times when you have to exert all of your energy. At such times, you should of course do your best. For example, a singer who holds back from doing his or her best when singing before a large audience will most likely get fired. People need to know when to perform at their best. Otherwise, you do not need to make an unnecessary display of yourself. If you act conspicuously like an animal that defensively bristles to scare others away, no one will approach you to give you advice, so you need to be careful about that.

On a daily basis, you should speak as frankly as possible, and keep an open mind to be able to listen to others. Thus, humility should not be a goal or moral virtue that one should aspire to achieve; you will naturally be humble if you truly want to develop yourself.

Truly capable people will never be neglected

The same can be said of movie stars. If they believe they are already well-established actors, they sometimes cannot grow any further. It is great to be cast in starring roles, but they should also be ready to take on any kind of role at any time.

In other jobs, too, you are not always assigned to a project that will get you in the limelight. You can be put in a position that is less desirable. That is when others are watching your patience and perseverance—how you behave, make an effort, or discipline yourself. These are watched not only by others but also by yourself; you will know these for yourself. The amount of effort you make during these times will often open a path for you to move on to the next stage.

In short, truly capable people are never neglected or forsaken. This is not the case for those who exaggerate their talents and skills; nor is it the case of a country or company that works to destroy itself by purging its talented people. Yet in circumstances where the people involved are naturally trying to develop and attain further growth, truly capable people are never left unattended. It is important to believe in this and to continue making an effort.

The effort to prevent oneself from being conceited

The Law of Cause and Effect might not always seem fair. People usually tend to be lenient with themselves and strict with others. It is natural that you sometimes become filled with frustration believing that your efforts are not rewarded. At such times, you need to shift your perspective and observe others.

Take, for example, an audition. Out of 5,000 candidates, only one can be selected for the Grand Prix winner. If you are the winner, you can give plenty of reasons why you believe you deserve it. But what about the remaining 4,999 people? Didn't they do their best? Do they really have less aptitude or less talent than you do? These factors remain unknown.

Even actors that play modest supporting roles could gradually gain popularity. This means that even though their talent is not obvious at first, it can sometimes take longer for greater talent to show. For this reason, it is better not to label yourself too easily. You should also be aware of the danger of achieving success too early. Being in the spotlight too early can later lead you to downfall.

Earlier, I mentioned my experience of being scolded by a manager. He warned me that even as I proudly sang in the spotlight, the audience might feel offended, kick the seats, or have left by the time I realized it. The people around me thought I was seeking attention, when in fact I had just thought I wasn't doing enough and had tried harder to do better. I have gone through such a period. You may have had a similar experience.

In general, you can clearly see others' weak points but hardly notice their good points. At the same time, you know your own strengths very well, but you want to hide your weaknesses or often try to avoid facing them.

People around you will not necessarily point out your weaknesses. They will choose to remain silent unless they trust you and feel safe to be completely honest with you. Without saying a word, sly people may even knowingly watch you from afar as you walk into your own demise.

Therefore, you should appreciate the fact that people give you warning or advice. Young people may feel hurt when their mistakes and errors are pointed out, but it is important to accept these comments with gratitude and try to use them as nourishment for further growth.

Your capability will grow
In proportion to your ability

It is not easy to grasp the mind. Even though it is your own, you might only understand it at the level of emotions, such as joy, anger, sorrow, and pleasure. Animals also have emotions. Even insects have slight emotions. How deeply you can perceive and recognize your mind as a real entity will show your growth as a human; this is the true nature of enlightenment.

Therefore, strive to develop the folds in your mind to be able to understand the feelings of different kinds of people. To be able to understand the feelings of many others means you have the ability to see different facets of your own mind. To this end, you need both intellectual discipline and physical effort.

What is more, you also need to undergo hardships that arise from human relationships. There are times when you have to assert your opinions that differ from those of others or times when you have to cooperate with others. You must sometimes make a courageous decision to lead others, or take responsibility for the outcome of your decision. At such times, your strong will to make a bold decision, or your courage, will also grow and develop. In other words, the range of decisions you can make, or the things you can get done, will expand along with your abilities and accomplishments. Please know this.

5

Make Efforts as You Remove Your Rust

✧　✧　✧

The Three Poisons of the Mind, Taught in Buddhism

Referring to the experience of my very first lecture, I self-reflected and saw how poorly I gave that talk. From then on, my lecture venues gradually became larger with greater audience attendance. The number of believers increased, and Happy Science expanded worldwide. In this sense, it is good to have a big dream. Even so, it is essential to make steady efforts and to advance step by step.

While there are life-long skills such as how to ride a bicycle, there are many others that we forget or lose. We must brush up on these skills to prevent them from being lost and continue making effort.

One of Shakyamuni Buddha's teachings is, "Rust eats away the very iron from which it is born." Rust is formed from iron. Products that contain iron work well at first, but when they are exposed to rain or get old, they rust. Swords covered with red rust do not cut. They are not usable unless they are polished and the rust is removed. The same is true for knives. Rust, which is born of iron, corrodes the iron and makes it unusable.

What is the equivalent of "rust" produced by humans? Simply stated, they are greed, anger, and foolishness, also called the Three Poisons of the Mind.

The first poison is greed. Do you have an excessive desire that surpasses your current or past achievement, efforts, or discipline? Check and see if you are greedy.

The second is anger. Are you short-tempered? When someone points out your errors, shortcomings, or failures, do you respond with rage?

Do you have extreme feelings of like or dislike, labeling things as good or bad based on your preferences? Do you judge people in the same way in romantic or workplace relationships as well? Such extreme emotions are deeply connected to anger. So, check and see if you have extreme emotions. Look fairly and squarely at others' strong and weak points. You will see that the differences between yourself and others are often rather small. So, if you find yourself with strong feelings of anger, practice self-reflection.

The third poison is foolishness. When you learn Buddha's Truth through books, you might think you understand it well. You could perhaps write an essay on the Law of Cause and Effect, for example, when requested to do so. However, some people would soon forget all they have studied after they finish their assignment and move on to do other things.

Your perspective will change
Through efforts and experience

You can develop a good eye or ear in proportion to your efforts, through which you will become able to judge many things. This is true in any line of work.

For example, I was watching a DVD the other day, a movie based on a novel by a well-known author. Many famous actors and actresses were cast and, with that kind of lineup, I expected it to be a masterpiece. In fact, the movie was poorly done and I was disappointed; I noticed several points that could have been made better. Then, I realized that my critical eye had become sharp because I too had been making movies.

In short, a filmmaker's perspective is different from that of someone who simply watches a movie for entertainment. Filmmakers notice many aspects of a movie, from the director's skills to the author's storyline to the actors' performances.

The movie was *Laplace's Witch*. My secretary bought the DVD for research since our film, *The Last White Witch* (Executive Producer and original story by Ryuho Okawa, February 2019 release) was under production. There were big names in the movie lineup, including Suzu Hirose and Sho Sakurai, a member of the J-pop group Arashi. The film was adapted from a novel written by a bestselling author. I was curious to see how a witch was depicted in the movie, but felt very let down at the end of it. It was indeed poor work.

The story had a modern touch, but there was nothing at all about a witch. Even with the big names among the cast, the ending was regrettable. In addition, one cast member was an actor I had praised for his great performances in all his work. But even his part came out very poorly. I thought the director had an "exceptional" skill to make this actor perform so terribly. The character he played died in so miserable a way that he did not show his true talent. This made me aware of the director's poor skills. It was rather shocking to find that I had developed such insight after having made movies myself. In spite of it all, the movie was somewhat successful, so I should not criticize it too much. Many good actors performed in the movie, and I do not want to cause any friction with them.

This was my experience of how I was able to spot flaws in a film I watched just to do research about witches. Of course, I must pay critical attention to my own work as well. Still, it is beneficial to know that experiences change a person's perspective.

I have discussed various topics in relation to the Law of Cause and Effect. I hope you will remember this Law from time to time. You might think that magic can make anything instantly possible, but remember, there is a cause for you to be able to use white magic, and a cause for you to come to use black magic. Please note that the Law of Cause and Effect also relates to magic in this way.

IN HARDSHIPS, GAIN BRILLIANCE OF THE SOUL AND VIRTUE

To acquire a strong mind,

It is necessary to discipline yourself

For a long time.

It is commonly believed that willpower is essential,

But willpower is not an innate quality.

People regard someone as having a strong will

By looking at their achievements.

No newborn baby is endowed with strong willpower,

Or mental fortitude, as a natural ability.

I am convinced that this ability is acquired

As we overcome life's various hardships.

Deep in your heart, you might naturally wish

To lead a comfortable and happy life

Without any ordeals or trials.

However, at some point in life,

A seemingly adverse situation will arise.

You may face unfavorable circumstances,

You may face many difficulties

Including setbacks in studies, failures at work,

Struggles or separations in personal relationships,

And experience hatred or sorrow.

You might wish in your heart

To avoid all such painful encounters.

But you cannot actually avoid them

Because evading such suffering and sorrow

Will make your soul training in this lifetime go to waste;

You will have to leave this world

Without undergoing any meaningful discipline,

Despite all your efforts to be born.

Some abilities or talents are indeed innate qualities,

But people cannot make progress

With those abilities alone.

The brilliance of the soul and virtue are born

As you struggle and overcome

The appropriate challenges of life

That are specifically designed for you.

So, here is my message:

For those who pray to avoid any hardship,

This is the same as you refusing to have virtue.

In hardship, you will gain the brilliance of your soul.

Therefore, be strong.

Be true to yourself.

Be humble before your Buddha-nature.

Strongly believe in your Buddha-nature.

Chapter THREE

FULFILLING
NOBLESSE
OBLIGE

Creating People and Nations that Can Produce
Value and Contribute to the World

Lecture given on May 3, 2018
at Tokyo Shoshinkan, Happy Science, Tokyo, Japan

1

Foreseeing the Effect of New Systems and Artificial Intelligence

The ultimate outcome of Japan's current work-style reform

In recent years, the number of public holidays has increased in Japan; in 2019, in particular, there were a longer number of consecutive days off due to the new emperor's enthronement. The Japanese government is now promoting work-style reforms,[*] but they do not make sense to me. While Japan already has more holidays than the United States, the government encourages people to leave work early on Fridays and is planning to build casino resorts where visitors will only be allowed to enter a maximum of three times a week. I do not really understand their intention.

The government has also pushed to raise the minimum wage and encouraged companies to increase salaries and employees' paid leave, while at the same time calling for more taxes. This makes

---

[*] Translator's Footnote: Work-style reform is the Japanese government's effort to improve working conditions to prevent work-related problems like *karoshi* (death by overwork) due to long working hours. The amendments to the Labor Standards Act that became effective on April 1, 2019 include companies' obligation to have their employees take at least five paid holidays a year and to set standards for a maximum limit on overtime work. Specifically, overtime is restricted to 720 hours per year. Companies that fail to abide by this regulation will face penalties. The amendment to the limit on overtime work for small- and medium-sized companies will take effect on April 1, 2020.

me wonder what the long-term outcome would be. These policies seem attractive to everyone from a short-term perspective while the current party is in power, but I have doubts about the ultimate result. Without a doubt, Japan will see a drop in its international competitiveness. I cannot help but interpret their message as encouragement for each citizen to lead the same lifestyle of four centuries ago during the Edo period, when people lived from hand to mouth without working or saving money, and even defaulting on debt. I find their "good intentions" somewhat peculiar and foreboding.

On the other hand, the government has also officially announced that the Japanese economy is continuing to improve, but in truth, people feel things are getting tighter and tighter financially. Although the government urges us to spend more of our savings, we cannot simply follow their advice, because this would only cause us to run out of money. After we have wasted money buying unnecessary things, we may end up having difficulty deciding what to do with them. I feel there is something wrong with their advice.

The condition that must be met to create talented people

In 2018, those who first studied under relaxed education policies[†] from elementary school through college entered the workforce.

Some have joined Happy Science as new staff members. While their abilities are still unknown, to be honest, I am a little afraid to find out.

I have not deeply researched the reformed curriculum, so I am not sure of the details, but it is clear that the content of current school textbooks has been cut by half compared to those used during my generation. Students spend an entire year learning half the content. This is very disconcerting. If the purpose of this is to allow them to rest from mental overwork, being weary of their studies at after-school cram schools, I suppose it is somewhat understandable. Providing free school education so that people can afford cram school fees also makes sense. But if so, the government will abandon its authority over educational matters, and must eventually become less involved in education.

In essence, education must be based on the relationship between self-motivated students who aspire to learn and teachers who are willing to respond to their drive. Advanced education must also be provided according to students' motivation. When students and teachers resonate with each other, I believe that talented people are fostered, and that great figures will emerge.

Nowadays, however, I am afraid that people see humans as things that can be produced uniformly, as if in a factory production line. This kind of view of humans seems to be spreading widely.

---

† TF: Relaxed education policies have been introduced in Japan in stages since the 1980s. Under these policies, the amount of class time and content of the educational curriculum have been gradually reduced.

Robots are certainly useful, and there is no doubt that artificial intelligence (AI) will be increasingly utilized to operate many things in the coming age. This seems to be a good thing, but at the same time a bad thing. The use of AI and robots will probably increase rapidly, and companies involved in related industries will make huge profits and widen their market share if they win out against competition. In unrelated sectors, it is highly likely that current jobs will be taken away, wages will be cut, and more people will have to wait for potential job openings.

Is a state-of-the-art function truly an evolution?

I used to have my own car for about 10 years, but later switched to leasing a car because I was told that the cost of repairs and maintenance was quite expensive—possibly as high as a million yen (about US$10,000) annually. The advice was that since the cost of repairs was so high, and new models with better functions came out every five years, it was not worth owning an older car.

I tried out my leased car for the first time when I went to Tokyo Shoshinkan. It felt like I was riding in a taxi. As I released my seat belt just before entering the parking lot, an alarm went off in the car, signaling that the seatbelts were off, like in a taxi. This may have been an improved function, but I thought it was too bothersome.

A taxi driver would quickly ask you to use the seatbelt, but there would be no problem taking it off just before readying to exit at your destination. I was confident it was safe because we were not on any highway, but the moment I took it off, the alarm sounded all around, which made me wonder if this could truly be called an advanced function.

Even a luxury car is not perfect; sometimes it is too noisy. It would be great if an alarm signaled danger, for instance, to wake a driver up when falling asleep at the wheel and kept silent otherwise. But that is not how it is. I had such an uneasy experience.

How will AI affect society, employment, and business?

I suppose that similar developments will be seen in many areas from now on. In this sense, a cyber society will eventually be created with the advancement of AI and other automations.

There is a positive side to this. In a simple way, it could help to reduce the number of employees to keep operational costs down, thereby stabilizing the company management. But seen from the opposite angle, this could inevitably lead to a drop in simple labor employment. Peering behind the government's intention in encouraging people to increase their number of holidays, it could also be interpreted that people should work only about half of the year, and instead increase temporary employment.

However, no matter how much the government wants to increase the number of holidays, some businesses like convenience stores cannot close up shop. General contractors and builders cannot easily take time off either because they have deadlines to meet. In order to do so, they sometimes have to hire more workers. Unless the government takes all possibilities into consideration and proceeds with these policies wisely and comprehensively, problems may well arise down the road.

2

Work that Has Spiritual Value Cannot Be Replaced by Robots

✧   ✧   ✧

AI technology has not sufficiently developed In language-related areas

While AI technology is still under development, it has now reached the level where it can win in contests against master players of shogi and go (Japanese board games). This is incredible. Young boys aspiring to become professional shogi players are excited by the game's rising popularity, but honestly speaking, the future prospects of shogi players are dim.

Nevertheless, areas remain that AI technology cannot sufficiently cover. Language, in particular, seems to be one such area. For example, I've heard that the English-language skills of AI have been enhanced enough to score over 900 points on the TOEIC[*] test, but this is the level that our students at Happy Science University[†] can achieve; more and more students now exceed 900 points after learning English from human teachers. Human

---

[*] TF: The Test of English for International Communication (TOEIC) is an international English proficiency test with a maximum score of 990 points.

[†] TF: Happy Science University is a private educational institution that opened in April 2015. See the end section.

brains cannot be undervalued; they are still superior to computers in some areas.

Regarding college entrance exams, AI has yet to reach the level needed to enter the best universities. While it can obtain high scores in mathematics, physics, and subjects that heavily rely on memorization, it remains less adapted to subjects like English and other linguistically related studies, which have flexible answers.

I have no intention of casting a shadow over the future of people doing engineering work in computers and AI technology. I hope that those engaged in these activities will develop better products through competition, thereby bringing a brighter future more quickly and achieving great success.

Jobs that only humans can do, not robots

On the other hand, people whose work are not related to these industries, those who are more likely in the position of potentially being replaced, will be forced to compete against machines. They need to add as much value as possible to their current work so as not to be replaced by robots or computers; otherwise, they cannot survive in the workplace.

Computers have now made inroads into Buddhist temples. Amazon Japan, for instance, now arranges the "home delivery" of services traditionally done by Buddhist priests. Sutras can be selected and recited by computers, and a posthumous Buddhist name can be presented in Chinese characters by typing the name and personal history of the deceased into a computer, thereby reducing fees to less than ¥300,000 (about US$3,000).

However, these changes undermine the spiritual value of Buddhist services and put the future of Buddhist temples at risk, though I might sound cold in saying this. There are many chief priests of Buddhist temples among Happy Science believers, and they recite their traditional sutras while studying my books. They need to be wary of this trend because their occupation could truly disappear.

In the future, there could be a robot simulating a priest's actions, tapping the wooden fish (block) and chanting sutras according to your requests. It may ask, "How would you like the sutra to be chanted? A little faster? If you wish for it to be done quickly, I can read an hour-long sutra in just 30 minutes. I can skip parts of it or chant it at double speed." This kind of service could be produced, but it is doubtful whether the true purpose of conducting religious memorial services could be fulfilled in this way.

We need a fresh review of work from this perspective: "What is essential to preserve spiritual value and fulfill our true purpose?" We cannot judge things based on how to simply reduce physical workload or cost.

What humans exceed at, for example, is coming up with new ideas. People innately have the power to find ideas. As mentioned earlier, computers lag behind in terms of linguistic ability. There are still many areas where humans excel over machines, such as producing novels and other written works, or making art like paintings and music.

Emotion-related fields are especially valuable. A large part of human jobs that serve to promote the stability, peace, and advancement of the human mind cannot be replaced by machines. Those who continue to improve their level of work in these areas will still have a way to survive in the future. Please keep this in mind.

Producing something noble
Through your life

This chapter's theme is "Fulfilling *Noblesse Oblige*." After having been born into this world as humans, it is very important to set a goal of how to live our lives. The purpose of our lives is definitely not just economic efficiency, simply cutting down expenses, or mechanically increasing the productivity of hourly work. We must work to elevate the way we live our lives. Average life expectancy has increased, but how to increase the "density" of time and live our lives to the fullest is extremely important.

How can you increase the "density" of time and live a fulfilling life? You need high aspirations. As long as you view humans like machines and believe that they evolved from amoebas and merely function as machines, which eventually break down and die, you can never create something noble. Therefore, it is essential to make an effort to seek out these spiritual values.

Work innately has the function of Creating something noble

At the beginning of this chapter, I talked about work-style reform. Listening to the arguments of the Japanese government, I have an impression that their idea is based on the concept that "labor is bad." According to the Judaic and Christian value systems, humans have to work hard as punishment from God; due to committing sin, they were expelled from the Garden of Eden, so that now women have to bear the pain of childbirth and men have to toil in sweat. Therefore, in the context of Western culture, work is somewhat akin to forced prison labor.

Japan, however, did not historically have this way of thinking and has no need to be affected by it. Work is a precious way of making your soul's time in this life shine brighter. It is very important to put your heart and soul into your work, and form something that will serve many people, and which can be passed on to future generations. You should not consider your work at a company similar to the forced labor of a prisoner. You cannot be happy that way.

Only a few jobs can be done individually, but it is more common for work to be carried out in collaboration with others, or as part of an organization. In these cases as well, if you put your soul into your work, it will be the source of joy for you and will lead to personal growth. At the same time, this joy and growth will be given back to society and in turn make others happy, thereby amplifying joy. You must imbue your work with spirituality and build such a society.

Work innately has the function of creating something noble. So, instead of viewing labor as fundamentally evil, aim to contribute to society more through work and to achieve happiness yourself. But while it is good that you become wealthy or gain a higher status or fame in the process, these aspects should be regarded as mere by-products.

In life, people aim to realize their goals through some kind of work, and it is crucial that their work not harm others, but benefit many. "I'm glad to have you in my life," or "Your work is very helpful" are words of appreciation we would like to hear from others. That is what we should live for, and what we should die for. It is fundamental that we be satisfied with the work we have done. Without this sense of noble duty, it would be difficult for humans to keep working over a longer period of time.

3
Preparing for the Age of 100-Year Life

✧   ✧   ✧

Reshaping your way of thinking and view of life

Now that the average life expectancy is estimated to increase to 100 years during the 21st century, companies are trying to extend the retirement age from 60 to about 65. But this shift will not come easily.

The truth is that how people spend their later years depends on their way of thinking. If they regard humans as similar to machines and believe they will only weaken with age, that is what will happen in the end. However, if they accept that life with an average lifespan of 100 years will soon be the norm, they will have to adapt to prepare for it. We must change our way of thinking and consider that we are not facing the end of life, but still have many years ahead.

The age of 50 would be the halfway mark, and your life would continue on. This being so, what would you do for the years to come? If you decide that 50 years is the halfway mark of your life, how would you spend the remaining 50 years? You need to make efforts to answer this question; otherwise, your life might well be extinguished like the flame of a match.

I give public lectures on the occasions of the Celebration of the Lord's Descent, as well as other events. Of course, it's not a painful work and I enjoy doing it, but recently I avoid mentioning my age or how long I have been doing my work, because when people mention them, it feels like my time is nearing its end. An increase in savings may well make a person happy, but an increase in age or the number of years that have passed in my work would not make me happy. So lately I try not to mention them.

I have already passed the average retirement age, but I do not feel I am done. When I am covered in the media, I am sometimes described as "of uncertain age," and I am fine with that. Life may be over for those who believe they are done. However, those who do not believe so will continuously have work to do.

What is needed to continue working? It is essential to constantly train to enhance your skills and abilities, while sowing and nurturing "seeds" of potential work. At the same time, regard the joy of others as your own, and make such a perspective on life your guiding principle.

Never giving in to the temptation of laziness

I have given many lectures, but sometimes I am tempted to think it might be better to give lectures less frequently to attract more listeners to each one. If I reduce my lectures to only once a month, for example, more people might attend each time. When this crosses my mind, I give it a second thought so as not to give in to such temptation; it would only make me lazy.

While I am now able to deliver over 100 lectures a year, if I lower that number to about 20, our local temples might have greater attendance at each lecture, making them appear livelier and more exciting. Some people might think this is a good idea, but I cannot accept it, because it would feel like spending five years to do the work I could do in one.

Therefore, I do what I must do. It is the work of my disciples to consider how to make the best use of my lectures and spread the teachings, how to give people who have yet to encounter the Truth more opportunities to experience my lectures. It is the disciples' mission to spread the Truth; I hope you will imprint this motto in your mind and carry it out as fully as possible.

If things are left as they are, only the same members would come to Happy Science local temples to watch my lectures and, with an increasing number of lectures, they would be unable to attend them all. So, we need to invite other people. Let others know what we offer and invite them to come watch my lectures for themselves. That is all we need to do. This is the work of the disciples, and I hope you will never be lenient on yourself.

HOW TO REJUVENATE YOURSELF 1
Be familiar with
The Happy Science philosophy and its community

There is a wide range of age groups among Happy Science believers, and a good thing about Happy Science is that both the young and old maintain youthful hearts to a certain degree. My philosophy has a rejuvenating effect on people of a certain age group.

There is also merit for younger people; they become able to develop mature ways of thinking. For this reason, when they begin working after they graduate from school, senior management might evaluate young people who have studied at Happy Science differently. Compared to their peers, who seem to have less knowledge because of a relaxed education, they probably stand out by showing substantial knowledge, and sometimes demonstrating management-level thinking for their age. Such outstanding young people are now emerging.

HOW TO REJUVENATE YOURSELF 2
Try to gain deep wisdom,
Rather than trivial information

What is needed to make a long life fulfilling and abundant? One thing is to have intellectual curiosity. Be continuously willing to learn something new and take interest in what you have yet to deeply understand. Aim to be able to speak or write something about it or present it to others or use it for new ideas.

There is virtually no all-knowing, all-capable person who is deeply versed in all fields of study. Young people today are called the "smartphone generation" and can obtain basic information through their smartphones. Honestly speaking, that level of information is not enough for people like me, whose work involves writing books or giving lectures in front of large audiences. Most people already know about the level of information accessible on a smartphone.

To give a lecture in front of a large audience, one must read materials that include academic books that are seldom read by others. One must also do research on various issues by reading as many sources as possible, not only in one's own language but also in foreign languages, even if they have not yet been translated.

So, strive to dig deeper. Today's society is abundant with trivial information that passes by quickly and soon disappears, like bubbles in a shallow current. Sometimes, those who are able to take in a large amount of such information in a short period of time are referred to as intellectual giants. But to me, they are not. They probably have a high "information processing ability," but this ability will definitely lose to the earlier-discussed AI technology and computers sooner or later.

These so-called intellectual giants might appear able to perform keen analysis compared to others, but they need to be determined and study each subject deeply; in this way, they need to elevate their knowledge to the level of wisdom. If they keep up with such efforts, they will most likely be able to continue working with clear minds even if the retirement age is extended from 60 to 65, 70, 75, or even 80.

HOW TO REJUVENATE YOURSELF 3
Try to stay fit, sometimes with the help of miracles

In addition, carefully do some physical training and control your health by occasionally and effectively taking a rest. Then, you will increasingly be able to stay active throughout your life, without needing to visit doctors or hospitals.

This may result in a decrease in the number of patients, and I apologize if there are doctors or hospital workers among my readers. Hospitals in Japan are now covered by numerous health care laws, enabling them to inflate their profits. That is why I think it is permissible for each individual to make some effort so as not to pay large medical bills. This is how you should think about it.

While medical science has gradually evolved, it tends to "create" illnesses that do not really exist, so we must be wary.

We sometimes present stories of healing in our Happy Science monthly magazines. The authorities might eventually start to monitor us, but fortunately, miracles do not happen to the extent that hospitals would go out of business. Miracles happen to the right people at the right time. If they occur everywhere, they are no longer miracles. This is why miracles only take place once in a while at different locations to awaken people to the Truth.

4
How to Receive Inspiration for Work

✧   ✧   ✧

Happy Science movies are inspired
By prominent authors now in heaven

No matter how much technology has advanced or how much information has increased in this world, there has been no increase in the type of information in which I am involved. Since I became engaged in religious activities around 1981, society has changed significantly, but has not been able to retrieve firsthand information on the other world.

Recently I received a spiritual message from the spirit of the late well-known Japanese author Ryotaro Shiba and heard his opinion on patriotism. He regretted that although there were many movies inspired by hell, there was no outlet for his inspirations. I could understand what he meant; there is no reason the spirit of Ryotaro Shiba should go about trying to offer his inspiration.

Happy Science Group also produces movies. Our books are basically non-fiction teachings, so if we want to make a film based on my books, we need a storyline. Since most of the books do not have a novel-like structure, we need to create an original story, which is equivalent to the main plot of a novel. I create them, and I wrote storylines for about 13 movies in 2018.

I have invented original stories, together with 40 songs, including each film's theme song, so that we can continue producing films up to the year 2024. I have already composed music that you will hear in a few years. This is how I usually work.

The spirit of Ryotaro Shiba visited me to give his spiritual message, also inspiring an original story for a movie. This is very valuable. This film is now approximately scheduled to be released in 2022 with the working title, *Aikoku-joshi* (lit. *"A Patriot Girl"*). It cannot be completed earlier due to our budget and the planned release of other movies.

The spirit of Ryotaro Shiba came down to me and inspired me to write the original story. When his spirit entered my body, I would sit in a chair facing slightly sideways, and wrote continuously, as if to complete a full-length novel. If I let him write as long as he wished, the movie will not end in two hours. I worried that he was intending to have me write so much every day, so at one point I decided to switch to recording the storyline until its completion.

In addition to Ryotaro Shiba, the spirits of other outstanding novelists like Ryunosuke Akutagawa and Soseki Natsume have also come to me from the heavenly world to inspire stories for our films, providing core storylines. The spirit of Yukio Mishima, another well-known author, has also come down.

Stories born in this way will be made into live-action films, which will eventually be shown in theaters in consecutive order. These movies will have considerable value. The body of work these writers produced while alive on earth of course has value, but our movies are based on inspirations these spirits have given me after accumulating further studies in the other world. Therefore, distinguished movies of immeasurable value will be coming out in the future.

On this matter, I doubt the computer world (AI) can produce such films. This is a kind of battle, but I am sure they cannot do it.

It is regrettable that I did not spend a lot on these writers' printed work when they were alive. If I were to buy it now, perhaps some of the royalties would go to the writers' living relatives, but obviously, the spirits do not earn anything. I'm sorry about that.

HOW TO RECEIVE INSPIRATION FOR WORK 1
Maintain a good state of mind

Many spirits in the higher realms of the heavenly world wish to help people on earth, and to send inspiration to anyone who they might want to help. These spirits are waiting to send inspiration in different ways in various fields, be they movies, novels, plays, manga, anime, music, or even new designs or fashions in clothing.

It all depends on our devotion and efforts in this world. If you attain a state of mind that moves these spirits to send you inspiration, they will certainly do so and give you advice. So, it is worthwhile to put effort into studying.

If you study the Truth at Happy Science, although I cannot say that everyone will become a buddha, you can become closer to Buddha, and higher spirits who formerly led respectable lives on earth as humans will start offering you advice. Then, you will receive an abundance of inspiration for whatever work you are doing. Compared to other companies in the same industry or other people with similar jobs, you will become very "inspirationable" and produce inspired work.

HOW TO RECEIVE INSPIRATION FOR WORK 2
Make an effort to develop your spiritual self

Even as you work while receiving inspiration, you cannot just expect it to keep coming. As I said earlier, with intellectual curiosity, continue diligent efforts to build yourself up, while training yourself little by little. Aspire to stay active as long as possible and aim to produce better outcomes in later years. Then, in all likelihood, that is how you will live.

In this sense, studying my lectures through books, CDs, and DVDs, and taking koan seminars at Happy Science are extremely important opportunities to establish a channel with the other world. I hope you will truly value these opportunities. We are now living in an age of low interest rates, so if you cannot think of a good use for your money, my advice would be to invest it to develop your spiritual self to open your future path.

HOW TO RECEIVE INSPIRATION FOR WORK 3
Aspire to be of service to others

Having said this, Happy Science does not just encourage personal self-realization. Please make no mistake here. You must first improve yourself and raise the level of your abilities, but these abilities will truly be your own only when they serve to help others. I always teach this way. I hope you will understand the importance of this attitude.

It is essential to foster a large number of people who have such noble spirits in Japan and all around the world. In this sense, we need to promote our missionary work, not only to gain authority or power as a religious group, but more importantly, to nurture many talented people who can support a future society that is affluent and highly spiritual. Please know that missionary work will be the power through which to realize this society.

Around the world, quite a few poor regions remain. I mentioned hospitals earlier, but there are many areas with no hospitals and not enough schools. Many people are unable to receive a sufficient education. There are many such countries.

We want to do something for these people, but in reality, we can hardly accomplish much because most of them are poor. Our efforts seem like trying to fill a bottomless pit that swallows everything up. Our International Headquarters cannot fill it with the current level of revenue.

In some countries, the individual average annual income per person is less than one hundredth that of Japan. When we go to such places to spread the Truth, we often end up spending more to distribute food than we receive in donations. We also print books on my teachings in local languages, but often end up distributing them for free. Though we want to spread the Truth as widely as possible, our efforts come to an impasse in some areas.

5
Reviewing Japan's "One Country Pacifism"

✧   ✧   ✧

The background behind
The creation of the Constitution of Japan

While understanding the world situation as stated above, it is important to contemplate the meaning of living in a currently peaceful country like Japan. After World War II, Japan has kept to the policy of "one country pacifism" for more than 70 years, but now a reconsideration of this policy is needed.

The lecture covered in this chapter was given on Japan's Constitution Memorial Day (May 3) but the heated debate over the revision of the Constitution had cooled down in recent times and people seemed to have lost interest in the issue (at the time of the lecture). This certainly cannot be helped, because the Japanese people have been believing, since the end of World War II, that as long as the current Constitution is preserved, Japan can enjoy peace and develop steadily.

However, looking at the current state of international affairs, circumstances have changed since the Constitution of Japan was enacted. When Japan was defeated in the war, it was undoubtedly seen as a country like the current North Korea. In this sense, the

Constitution of Japan was created to prevent it from ever again daring to defy the world. As far as I can understand, the purpose of the rigid Constitution of Japan, which renounces war and prohibits war potential, is to make sure Japan would never be able to fight back.

Japan has been a democratic country Longer than the U.S.

Japan was able to overcome such adversity and build a prosperous nation after the defeat in World War II. This was all due to the great efforts of those Japanese people who lived through the postwar period. Japanese people were traditionally diligent, and this spirit of the Japanese people had returned to life after the war.

In the first place, among the U.S. administrators who had come to write the Constitution of Japan, there were probably many who believed that the defeat would finally bring democracy to Japan. In reality, however, since the Meiji Constitution had been enacted in 1889, parliamentary democracy was already in place. Even before that, the 1867 Meiji Restoration aimed to achieve equality for all people, abolishing the then-existing four classes of society. In this context, Japan was more advanced than the U.S.

In the U.S., the African-Americans were still discriminated against during the time of President Kennedy, who had tried to solve the issue; however, he was assassinated while visiting the South where discrimination was strong. Even in the 1960s, African-Americans were the first soldiers sent to the battle lines and dangerous war zones during a war. In those times in the U.S., segregation on public transportation, in schools, and even in bathrooms was still common. This was when President Kennedy tried to reform the social structure.

In comparison, Japan's effort to seek equality of all people during the Meiji Restoration was much more advanced. In this context, Japan was already a civilized country at that time. Japan has maintained a high level of culture since the Heian period in the 8th century or perhaps even before that. I believe the Japanese people should properly acknowledge this and be more confident about its positive aspects.

Happy Science has been calling for North Korea's bloodless surrender

With this information in the background, I will now briefly speak about what would be the ideal states for Japan and its surrounding countries. In April 2018, an inter-Korean summit was held, giving an impression there was a sudden move to realize peace. The increased media coverage also reinforced such an impression. There were even some reports that North Korea's leader Kim Jong-un and South Korea's leader Moon Jae-in were the most likely candidates to win the 2018 Nobel Peace Prize. I was puzzled by such reporting.

Kim Jong-un, who had threatened the U.S. by launching ballistic missiles the year earlier, had sent his sister (Kim Yo-jong) to the PyeongChang Winter Olympic Games in 2018. On seeing that her visit was positively received, he made a sudden shift in strategy to talk about denuclearization to achieve peace. But we should not be fooled by his actions so easily. It is hard to believe that someone who had long worked to develop atomic and hydrogen bombs and even boasted to wage war against the U.S. using intercontinental ballistic missiles a year earlier would make an abrupt change. The only reason for this would most probably be either it is the only way for him to survive due to critical domestic conditions or he is planning something worse.

My hope certainly is that peace is achieved through negotiation, without having to go to war. I am totally in favor of that. At a special event lecture in 2017[*], I called for North Korea to consider peaceful bloodless surrender. I am still calling for its

---

[*] TF: On August 2, Okawa gave a public lecture titled, "The Choice of Humankind," in Tokyo Dome. Refer to Chapter Six of *The Laws of Faith* (New York: IRH Press, 2018).

complete renouncement of nuclear weapons and missiles, and do not necessarily uphold the idea of winning through war.

Points to distinguish a true leader from a dictator

We need to discern the nature of a sovereign leader. Are they a dictator, or a truly capable, indispensable leader who can unite people? It is essential to make this distinction. The difference is whether a supreme leader would demonstrate a self-sacrificing spirit at crucial times, whether they would be willing to sacrifice their own lives to save their people. Having the spirit of self-sacrifice clearly shows the difference between a hero and someone who is not.

I am afraid this may sound like boasting about Japan, but at the end of World War II, Japan's Emperor Hirohito (known posthumously as Showa) came before General MacArthur in person to ask him to save the Japanese people no matter what would happen to him. MacArthur was so impressed that he later remarked he had seen a god-like gentleman.

I am not sure if MacArthur meant the praise or was giving lip service, but Emperor Showa had certainly acted in a way that a dictator would never do. He humbly requested something like, "My people are suffering from starvation, so please help them. It doesn't matter what will happen to me." Emperor Showa most probably thought that going to General MacArthur at the General Headquarters (GHQ) could lead to his arrest and execution. There must have been many in the GHQ who supported the idea of arresting the Emperor and giving him a public execution. Even in such circumstances, Showa Emperor bravely went to see MacArthur alone to ask him to save his people in exchange for his life. I think this is one of the reasons why the Japanese Imperial Household was allowed to remain after the war.

The question is whether Kim Jong-un shares the same sentiment. If he says, "I will denuclearize my country regardless of what happens to me. So, please save my people. Please do not destroy the civilian population," then he will gain approval and may deserve the Nobel Peace Prize. However, if he does not have such an altruistic heart and just wants to prolong his life for now, then it is a problem.

6

The Duty to Save People
From Aggressive Authoritarian Countries

✧   ✧   ✧

How should North Korea
Proceed with disarmament?

What is important is not the mere removal of the dictator. Even if he is dismissed, the military can then establish a military dictatorship without revealing individual faces, and that becomes another obstacle. For this reason, I hope President Trump would strive to achieve not only denuclearization but at the same time the complete disarmament of North Korea by having it abandon its long-, mid- and short-range ballistic missiles, chemical and bio-chemical weapons, or anything that would result in devastating warfare.

President Trump is scheduled to meet with Kim Jong-un for a U.S.-North Korea Summit. (Note: On June 12, 2018, the first U.S.-North Korea Summit was held in Singapore.) I hope he will not be content with Kim Jong-un's empty promise of denuclearization, nor be deluded by any expression like, "We'll make an effort" or "We'll proceed step by step."

The potential summit meeting sites were Ulaanbaatar (Mongolia) or Singapore, but recently President Trump suggested Panmunjom as an alternative, where the earlier inter-Korean Summit took place. In my view, his wish to meet in Panmunjom indicates he is making preparations for either outcome, peace or war.

In April 2018, Kim Jong-un visited South Korea. To keep the South Korean people from being fooled by North Korea's friendly gestures, the American leader must have strong determination when stepping into Panmunjom to achieve total disarmament of North Korea based on the shared values of the U.S.-South Korea alliance. At the same time, his visit would most probably have another purpose—encouraging the U.S. troops stationed in South Korea, as well as the U.S. Marine Corps. In case the talks should fall apart, the U.S. would be able to swiftly begin preparation for war.

Before President Trump sets foot in Panmunjom, the Seventh Fleet would be in place for his protection. Given that, I assume that the U.S. is determined to press North Korea to choose either destruction by military force or agreeing to complete disarmament. (Note: One year after this lecture, on June 30, 2019, President Trump visited South Korea after having attended the G20 Summit in Osaka, and met with Kim Jong-un at the demarcation line in Panmunjom without any prior notice and held the third U.S.-North Korea Summit.)

The tragedies of oppressed regions: South Mongolia, Xinjiang, and Tibet

Be reminded that North Korea is not the only issue. Next comes the problem of China. South Mongolia (Inner Mongolia Autonomous Region) remains under Chinese occupation, while the rest of Mongolia also faces harsh conditions.

Happy Science carries out missionary work in Mongolia as well, and since there is no local temple there, about a dozen followers gather in an open field to hold meditation seminars under the open skies. Although small in scale, they spread the Truth and publish my books in Mongolian.

The Xinjiang Uyghur Autonomous Region is another place that suffers. As the Happiness Realization Party leader Ryoko Shaku strongly protests, Uyghurs have been severely oppressed under China's cultural assimilation plan ever since they were occupied. They seem to be suffering very harsh conditions.

According to some sources, there have been cases of organs of detained Uyghurs being sold, and one to two million Uyghurs have been either killed or deprived of freedom by detention in concentration camps. The Xinjiang Uyghur Autonomous Region, which native Uyghurs call East Turkestan, is mainly inhabited by Muslims. Since religion is considered opium in Marxist philosophy, China probably feels it has good reason to oppress these people.

Other than these regions, Tibet was also suddenly occupied by China in 1950; this was depicted in the movie *Seven Years in Tibet*. Taiwan, too, is now facing such a crisis. The Philippines are not safe either. China has attempted to take over these regions as a hegemonic state, and has actually done so.

Introducing freedom, democracy, and faith Into China's political system

My message for China is clear. The direction which Chinese politics should aim to take and the values China should hold are freedom, democracy, and faith. These three elements must be introduced into China's political system, and this is what China must aim to achieve in the future.

An authoritarian state will automatically collapse with the introduction of freedom and democracy. These elements would allow a variety of values to arise and compete with one another in the country, so there would be no need to use missiles to bring down the government; it would only take the introduction of freedom and democracy into China's political system.

Then, finally, faith and religious freedom must also be introduced. A country governed by a dictator tends to have many bad laws. The authority creates laws to make the country appear like a constitutional state, and uses these laws to purge people and does whatever the central figure wants. But the truth is that these are bad laws, and they are rampant. That is why faith is indispensable. Justice needs to stand above what is made by humans. By preserving religious freedom, human rights will have true meaning for the first time.

In East Asia, no country is now able to stand against China that dares to take over the territories of others. This is the ongoing situation. We must increase our influence, with Japan as a pivotal base, to urge China to take up freedom, democracy, and faith as important political values, or to guide it to shift in that direction.

In Muslim countries, too, there are dangerous areas under the influence of Al Qaeda or the Islamic State (IS). However, as Ms. Malala Yousafzai has said, I believe that 90 percent of Muslim countries have the potential to accept a democratic political system. By learning the teachings of Happy Science, I think the obstinate thinking of Muslim people can be eased and their understanding will increase.

I truly want to accomplish all these things, so please allow us to have five or ten times more power. This concludes the chapter on "Fulfilling *Noblesse Oblige*."

A Small Enlightenment that Leads Individuals and Organizations to Success

The secret of success,

Whether you are a small business or a large company,

Is to restrain your ego and

Consider what can be done to benefit other people

Instead of benefiting yourself,

Which is a natural way for humans to think.

This is shown in the saying of Sontoku Ninomiya:

"If you try to gather hot water to yourself in a bathtub,

It will flow away in the opposite direction.

But if you push it away from yourself,

It will flow around and come back to you."

This is indeed the secret to doing business.

If your action is based on a desire to benefit yourself,

Both people and money will go away.

Rather, restrain your desires and think of other people.

When you start thinking about how to benefit others,

Goodwill will sometimes come back to you.

This is the basic starting point of running a business.

People who cannot change to such a mindset

Can hardly utilize others to establish a business,

Though they may get by with their own specialized skills.

To be able to do this, you need to transform yourself.

Since you have to restrain your ego

And share happiness with others,

Changing your way of thinking is very difficult.

If you want to further expand your business,

You need to listen carefully

To each customer complaint, criticism,

And negative comment.

Some people may run a business

Strongly craving important status

Or other people's praise.

But even if that is all they aim for,

Their wishes will not always be fulfilled,

Because not everyone will praise you and comfort you.

When customers become angry or complain to you,

Sincerely accept your fault in each case,

Find a solution and provide a better service or product,

And continue to make efforts to be of service to others,

Then you will be able to develop your business

And receive the respect of others without seeking it.

I believe this is one little enlightenment.

Those who are unable to grasp this truth

Can never be good business executives.

Chapter FOUR

BE CONFIDENT
IN YOUR LIFE

*Build the Kingdom of the Mind and
Spread the Design of the World's Future*

Lecture given on July 5, 2019
at Fukuoka Kokusai Center, Fukuoka, Japan

1

How to Become Impassioned
To Succeed at Work

The Celebration of the Lord's Descent
Broadcast by satellite in countries around the world

The lecture for the 2019 Happy Science Celebration of the Lord's Descent was given in Fukuoka, Kyushu, Southern Japan. This was quite unusual, possibly the first and last time to hold such an event in Kyushu. I would be happy if those who attended my lecture would remember it as a special event in their lives.

I have usually given the commemorative lecture for the Celebration of the Lord's Descent in the vicinity of Tokyo so people can easily gather from all over the country. But in the summer of 2019, there was an upcoming national event (the 25th House of Councilors election), and since the election date was not yet fixed, we could not determine the date for the lecture either. Our staff did not book a venue in advance and had planned to hold the event at a small venue, but I demanded that they search nationwide to secure a large hall, no matter where it was.

Our schedule for the Celebration of the Lord's Descent was thus pending until the election date could be decided. So, as July approached, I made the staff find any available event hall. They found two possible locations: Fukuoka and Tokushima. Since I had aired a lecture at a large venue in Tokushima a few years before, I decided on Fukuoka this time.

The Celebration of the Lord's Descent was broadcast by satellite to countries around the world, so our overseas audience might have wondered why Fukuoka was chosen. For Japan, Fukuoka is a base for dispatching information to Asia and is also the place of defense, so my speech from Fukuoka had some meaning.

Aside from that, I was concerned about the heavy rainfall that had continued for some time in the Kyushu region. It had stopped when I arrived in Fukuoka and I felt some relief.

Strong confidence can open a way for you

Since the lecture in this chapter is also intended for people around the world, I will try to avoid any detailed technical matters to make it easier for everyone to understand and to keep to the subject of my message, "Be Confident in Your Life."

"Be confident in your life" is a topic that many people have spoken on, and strong confidence can indeed open up a way for you. This lecture was originally given on the occasion of the Celebration of the Lord's Descent on July 5, 2019, marking my

2,950th lecture, and the number will soon reach 3,000[*]. Doing this would be impossible without confidence. I am determined to succeed in all I attempt, and have maintained this attitude in nearly 3,000 lectures.

We never know what may happen before I give my lectures; many unexpected things always occur. They often happen suddenly. In some countries, there were dangerous places where guards had to be armed for protection. In other places, I could not get enough sleep the day before my lecture. When I went to India, I thought it would be hot, but the air conditioning in the hotel was set so low that I shivered with cold.

So, many things happen. After holding thousands of lectures, we have experienced all sorts of environments and situations. When I gave a lecture in Ehime Prefecture, on Shikoku Island, I headed to the venue while a typhoon was approaching there. However, it turned out that the typhoon did not come during my morning lecture but hit later that day.

When I gave a lecture in Aomori Prefecture in Northern Japan, it was soon after the North Korean missiles flew over the Tsugaru Strait and the residents were afraid. So I decided to go there with strong resolve as though I could shoot the missiles down using my supernatural power. It does not cost anything to use supernatural power, so it might be an economical way to solve

---

[*] TF: On September 29, 2019, Okawa gave his 3,000th lecture when he recorded "Spiritual Message from Sayyid Khomeini [2]".

the issue. Of course, we cannot use this approach all the time, but we cannot hold lectures if we have fear in us.

Thus, we have done our best under any such circumstance, despite difficult situations or unexpected events. We have kept this attitude for these 33 years since the founding of Happy Science.

Giving a lecture to an audience of 8,500 people
At the age of 33

A few days before I gave the lecture in Fukuoka, I listened again to some of the lectures I had given in my first three years after having founded Happy Science—around the time I was 30 to 33 years old. I feel that my lectures were very impressive back then too if I may say so myself; I did well even when I was only 30 years old.

I tried hard when I was 60 and will try hard even at 63, but I was also doing well when I was 30. My Kansai accent was much stronger in those days compared to now, but my lectures were good even when I was 30 to 33 years old. At the age of 33, I had already given a lecture to an audience of about 8,500 people at the Ryogoku Kokugikan arena. It was commented that I had nerves of steel; I guess I was confident.

In 2004, however, I had almost died as depicted in the movie, *Immortal Hero* (Executive Producer and original story by Ryuho

Okawa, released in October 2019). In this sense, the year 2019 was the 15th anniversary of my resurrection, as well as the 33rd anniversary of the founding of Happy Science.

Factors of success:
A sense of mission, passion, and confidence

It is certainly a very happy situation to be able to work. It is very important that one has something to do. "I still have important things to do. There are things I must do in this world. There are messages I must convey to people. There are things I have yet to complete"—these thoughts will turn into your sense of mission and passion, and inflame your motivation.

Before my Fukuoka lecture, I had heard that Kyushu was a place of passion, and all I needed to do there was to inflame people's passion, rather than give some difficult speech. I had also heard that in Kyushu, whenever Happy Science members met, they would just remind each other of their passion. They value passion over love, wisdom, self-reflection, or progress.

They are, in a way, right. With passion, you can do anything. With passion, you can accomplish much more than average in any job. If you have a strong conviction and continue your work, you can succeed in anything without exception.

For example, on the way to my lecture venue in Fukuoka, I saw some food stalls selling food like ramen noodles. Even if you started out working from a stall, if you work hard with a burning passion to develop your business, you will certainly be able to open a ramen shop, then into a large business, and be successful. This is possible in any occupation.

Appreciation for what you have been given And the willingness to give back to others

You may not feel confident about many things, such as your current ability, or your past career and achievements, but it is no good just fretting over negative factors. Instead, appreciate what you now have, and you will realize how much you have been given. You have been given so much and this is something to be truly grateful for.

If I were asked to point out just one weakness in modern people, it would be their lack of gratitude. They just think about receiving rather than giving. Feeling gratitude and wanting to give back to others—these feelings are lacking. With the feeling of gratitude and the willingness to give back to others, you can open up any path no matter what you do, and people around you will also come and help you. This is very important.

Do not limit yourself
By your inherited qualities or past achievements

I gave my first lecture in 1986 at the Happy Science Launch Commemoration Session and then started to continually give public lectures from 1987. That was 33 years ago.

After hearing my lecture in those days, my father once commented that no one would come to my lecture since there was nothing good about me; he said my voice was bad, my looks were bad, my style was bad, and I could not be smart as I was the offspring of my mother and father. Those were certainly the qualities I inherited from my parents. But it is up to each of you how you polish your inherited qualities with your own efforts and turn them into something beneficial and into your strengths.

So, do not limit yourself only to your natural disposition, inherited traits from your parents, or your past achievements. As long as you keep going, you will advance much further than you ever imagined.

I feel this strongly, particularly from the work I do. The further I progress, the more I notice as I look back and think, "Ah, how small the scale of my thoughts was," "How little my confidence was in myself," "How little faith I had in my abilities," or "How unsure I was of the potential support of the people around me."

2
Words and Energy Will Change
Your Surroundings and the World

Mystical power
To transform reality and draw supporters

You must move forward resolutely and be determined to accomplish things to the very end, even if there is no one to help you. If you have such a strong resolve, other people will certainly be drawn to you and join you. On the contrary, if you lack confidence in yourself, you will receive all sorts of criticism, negative comments, or be told to stop doing stupid things.

So, be confident and have a strong will to keep pushing forward. Then, reality will be bound to change around you and people will come to support you. This is quite amazing.

When I decided to engage in my religious calling while still working at a company, for example, I assumed that no one would support me. I strongly felt that I had to set out alone. I did not want to rely on my friends; rather, I was determined to do this work alone when I started Happy Science.

However, soon I found that many people, even those I had never met, began to give me their support and help me; they were from all around the country. In this way, we grew larger. I am filled with amazement as to how many people are seeking the Truth.

Happy Science is now working simultaneously on several projects in progress. Considering how I started from zero, we can say we have achieved a certain degree of success in a number of them. As we continue these, we are still trying to launch other related projects. We are thus trying to achieve further growth as we head into the future, and we need not worry about anything.

Our final goal in Japan is to make Happy Science a state religion. If we have such a goal, we can do anything. There must always be something we can do to get closer to this goal. While we have such a goal, we should not stop there because there are also people overseas who study my lectures. We must make Happy Science a world religion.

There is no way that we, who aspire to make Happy Science a world religion, will fail to accomplish any work that we set our hearts on. Absolutely no way. We must absolutely grow stronger and stronger, and bigger and bigger year after year, and persist in our aspiration. In that sense, we must not remain small-minded.

The light and power of the universe
Will unlock your potential

The House of Councilors election was drawing closer when I gave this chapter's lecture, so I was given several restrictions for speaking in public, which made it a little difficult for me. I was limited to my position as the Master and CEO of Happy Science Group, rather than the founder and president of the Happiness Realization Party (HRP, see end section), the political organization.

Most people do not have any experience as politicians, so they may well think that politicians are great people who do a difficult job. They may feel there is a huge wall between politicians and themselves. But when I happened to see a Diet member sitting near me on my way to Kyushu, she was wearing sneakers and walking casually. It did not appear to me as if she was engaged in such a difficult job. She is a former singer who became popular in her early teens. This made me think that success as a singer is all it takes to become a Diet member.

I am certainly not downplaying her; we are also trying to produce many good singers of our own. We even have a singer who made his debut at the age of 40, which is quite admirable. He also acted in the role of the main character, myself, in our movie, *Immortal Hero*. I might have to dress up a bit more and perhaps should wear a white outfit as he does in the future.

You never know what happens in life. Some people become actors or singers for the first time at the age of 40, while others become politicians after a long career in some other job. There are also religious leaders who become politicians. Many things can happen in this way. These people, who have accumulated various life experiences, should eventually become leaders. This is very important.

So, stop limiting yourself as being small. Everyone has great potential. This potential will be unlocked when you open your heart and receive more and more light of the universe flowing into you.

Strive to fulfill your mission as a child of God or child of Buddha, and you will become a different person, so different that even you may not recognize yourself. You will think, "I didn't realize I was this smart and passionate," "I can't believe that such wonderful words came out of my mouth," "It's amazing how many people trust in me," or "I didn't know I had such an influence on people."

The future will truly change day by day and moment by moment. It is extremely important to make sure that you change it in a better direction.

Sometimes, you may be able to achieve only 1 percent of what you set out to achieve, but if you continue holding your goal in mind, that 1 percent will gradually build up to 2, 3, 5, 10, 20 percent, or more. Without a doubt, it will happen. So, do not think of yourself as small. Even though you are a limited being, the power in the universe is tremendously great.

In a lecture I gave in the early days of Happy Science, I once said that if I describe El Cantare (see end section) visually, it is a mass of light 10 km (about 6 miles) in diameter. Something 10 km wide would be hard to fit in a human body, so actually, it would be proportionate to only the tip of a match. But although I said that, the truth is that it is much bigger than just 10 km, given that it encompasses the entire Earth and visits different planets of the universe to give guidance. It must have much greater power to do that. I now think it was just a modest description.

We are affecting Japan, Hong Kong, Taiwan, and the world

My teachings have extended into various fields and built up to such a great extent that I can now voice my opinions on how Japan should be and how the world should be. In the beginning, my remarks may have sounded unrealistic, but the opinions I voice at present are about how Japan should head into the future and which direction the world should now take.

Things have really been changing. Look at Hong Kong. One million people rallied in protest, then two million. Happy Science and the HRP are the only groups in Japan that are supporting them. We proactively support them, and they know that. They are asking for help from Japan. Before that, I went to Taiwan and it too has now become a high-spirited and strong-willed nation.

I am not encouraging countries to argue or fight with each other. We think about what each country should do to make its people shine brighter and be happier, and when we decide that a certain direction is better, we support that idea. We do not fixate on any particular ideology or ways of thinking and then tell people to do everything in accordance with that. Rather, we consider each person's well-being and the happiness and future of each country, and then suggest what people should do.

3
The U.S. President Trump's Policies are Akin to the Happiness Realization Party's

Foreseeing Mr. Trump's abilities

Three years ago, there was the presidential election in the United States. At that time, people were saying that Mr. Trump had no chance of winning. However, I predicted that he would become president, and encouraged an aide of his. The aide had read my book on the spiritual interview with Mr. Trump's guardian spirit in English*, but even so, he was not convinced of Mr. Trump's victory and was not confident. But in the end, Mr. Trump won.

The mass media was certainly very critical and it still is, but it seems to me that Mr. Trump has gradually been displaying his true abilities and achieving success. I now feel I was right in my judgment.

---

* TF: Refer to Chapter Four of *The Trump Secret: Seeing Through the Past, Present, and Future of the New American President* (New York: IRH Press, 2017).

The Happiness Realization Party is equivalent To the U.S. Republican Party

There is a book titled, *Trumponomics* (coauthored by Stephen Moore and Arthur B. Laffer). It is about Mr. Trump's economic policies, written by his former advisers. We have connections with them, and we are currently under negotiation to acquire the rights to translate the book.* We are planning to introduce some quotes of the content together with the translation in our *Kuro-obi English* (lit. "Black Belt in English") series (published by Happy Science), in one of *Kuro-obi 10 Dan*, and are determined to acquire the translation rights.

People in the HRP have obtained an excerpt of the Japanese translation and studied it. Since *Trumponomics* has yet to be officially published in Japanese, most Japanese people probably do not know its contents, but they are almost the same as what we have been saying for the last 10 years since we founded the HRP. Mr. Trump became president after the 2016 presidential election, but we have been stating these ideas since 2009. It almost seems as if he has followed our opinions.

Of course, he probably is not imitating us. However, since we almost have the same source of inspiration, we come to have the

---

* TF: After the lecture, Happy Science had successfully acquired the translation rights for *Trumponomics*; its Japanese translation with the same title was published around the end of December 2019.

same sort of ideas. The policies advocated by the HRP are unique in Japan and may sound questionable to many Japanese people. However, according to the "source" of Mr. Trump's inspiration, the same kinds of inspiration have been given to Japan and the U.S.

Japan does not have two major parties like the Republicans and Democrats in the U.S. In the past, there was no political party in Japan that resembled the U.S. Republican Party.

Japan has the Liberal Democratic Party (LDP), which has long been in power. Although some people may consider it to be hawkish, it actually is not. Prime Minister Abe is not a hawk, but more like a dove. The LDP is leaning more and more toward the left. It incorporates similar policies proposed by left-wing parties like the Japanese Communist Party and the Social Democratic Party.

So, the current LDP is equivalent to the Democratic Party in the U.S., and the U.S. Republican Party would be the same as the HRP in Japan.

In Japan, the leaders of the opposition parties also take part in discussion forums on TV, but Japan's existing opposition parties would be considered minor parties in the U.S. The U.S. has no political party that advocates stubborn ideas like preserving the current constitution. All parties are more concerned about how to make new changes. But Japan has many politicians who are like obsolete "protected species," and they lead the opposition parties.

Japan has no Diet members who correspond to the U.S. Republicans. The Republicans are so-called "conservative," aspiring for a strong America. They also aim for a smaller government, aspiring to achieve economic growth to make America strong again and bring order to the world. This is the idea of the U.S. Republicans.

Only the HRP in Japan advocates similar ideas that represent the global mainstream viewpoint, but less than 1 percent of Japanese people share this view. The reason is that the commonly accepted knowledge of the Japanese people, the mass media, and what is taught in education are completely wrong. We need to change people's ways of thinking.

The ideas proposed by the HRP can make someone a president of the U.S. Our views are right; there is no mistake about them. If you read *Trumponomics*, you will see that the book has mostly the same ideas as those of the HRP.

The U.S. economic growth rate has risen After Mr. Trump's corporate tax reduction

Furthermore, the HRP also aims to reduce the consumption tax to 5 percent, instead of raising it from 8 to 10 percent. Many other parties also opposed the tax hike, and some may think that we were simply talking about the tax hike scheduled for the fall of 2019. The opposition parties were certainly just referring to the upcoming tax hike. The Japanese Communist Party even spoke of taking a huge tax bite from those firms that had made large profits to distribute to the poor.

According to Trumponomics, however, Mr. Trump's idea was not aimed at having just a short-term effect. He clearly stated that he would lower the corporate tax from the maximum rate of about 35 percent to about 15 percent, regardless of the size of the company. By doing so, he was aiming for the U.S. to boost and develop its economy by gaining international competitiveness.

According to his idea, lowering the tax rates would work to boost the economy because companies would be motivated and increase investment while consumers would also increase their spending with expectations of a brighter future. This is already happening in the U.S. During the Obama administration, the U.S. economic growth was about 1.6 percent, but it has gone over 3.1 percent after Mr. Trump took office and he is aiming to increase it to 5 percent.

4

The Happiness Realization Party's Future Design of Japan

✧   ✧   ✧

Tax reduction will increase The economic growth rate

Many people may argue that reducing the consumption tax from 8 percent to 5 percent will only expand the fiscal deficit, but that is not our intention. Our policies include reviewing the corporate tax rate and the inheritance tax rate. These tax reductions will help to improve the overall Japanese economy, and by developing the economy, we can increase the total tax revenue. In addition, as the economy expands, we can resolve all other problems including the pension issue.

The HRP leader Ryoko Shaku says that the pension problem can be resolved if the Japanese economic growth rate reaches 4.1 percent. I do not know how she reached this conclusion, but this figure must be right because she is very intelligent. Although I have not verified it myself, my intuition tells me it would be true.

The Japanese economy has long been in a sluggish state, but it is about time we turned this situation around. To keep an economy stagnant for 30 years is far beyond human ability, even God cannot do it. Japan has continued in this seemingly impossible state for the last 30 years, only managing to increase its economy by 1.5 times during that period. This is a terrible situation; any measures would work to achieve higher economic growth.

My idea to deal with this issue is by tax reduction. Rather than being dependent on a big government to support our lives, I would encourage companies to boost their business and consumers to increase their spending, thereby expanding the size of the economy. The Japanese economy has been stagnant for 30 years, so once we open a path, it is certain to expand. This is what we want to do.

We want to start by first achieving 3 percent economic growth and then increase it to 5 percent. This is almost the same as the ideas of Trumponomics; 5 percent economic growth is our goal.

On Japan overtaking China's GDP by 2050

In terms of macroeconomics, we want Japan's GDP to overtake China's by 2050. This is our basic idea, and Japan deserves to be in that position.

It is hard to believe that in the last 30 years, the Chinese economy has increased by 75 times, while the Japanese economy only increased by 1.5 times. Who could have managed the country so poorly to cause such a long stagnation? I want to see their faces, though I already know who they are.

However, the statistics of China are somewhat questionable; there seems to be much falsification involved, and the truth will be revealed soon. They claim to have maintained more than a 7 percent annual economic growth rate, but it seems to have dipped below 7 percent in 2015. It has even been reported to have a growth rate of 6.6 percent for 2018.

According to the calculations made by a certain expert, however, China's economic growth rate in 2018 was only 1.67 percent. He also estimates that China has already begun to have negative economic growth and I think this estimate is rather closer to the truth. I feel the economic bubble has already started to fall apart in China.

So, what Japan must do now are as follows: put its economy back on track to grow and revitalize the country; and develop righteous opinions and ways of thinking to be able to lead the world and clearly speak out about what is right and wrong to achieve world justice. At the very least, Japan must have an important influence on Asian countries, and show an ideal image of the future.

Furthermore, it is essential to clearly design the ideal image for what Japan's relationship should be with the U.S., Russia, and Europe. This is what the HRP, Japan's Republican Party, is considering.

Mass media does not need
To highlight coverage of one-issue parties

Japan has a very narrow range of thinking. Japanese election campaigns are often based on single-issue politics with candidates just focusing on one attention-grabbing topic to win an election.

On the day of the public announcement for the House of Councilors election (July 4, 2019), I watched NHK reporting the first election campaign speeches of various party leaders. They even reported on the speech of the leader of the anti-NHK party, the Party to Protect the People from NHK, twice. I do not know why they engage in this form of self-harm; I cannot see any reason why NHK should report it. Perhaps they broadcast it to show their fairness, but since the majority of people do not regard that party's assertion as worthwhile, there is no need to report it.

Only NHK constantly covers news that does not contribute to its ratings, such as continuous reports about heavy rains causing floods in certain local areas and the resulting casualties. They do such unprofitable work to serve the public interest regardless of their ratings, so they should be more confident in what they do. They definitely do not need to cover a party that only focuses on a single issue. Instead of reporting such a party, I suggest that NHK broadcast more about a better political party, Japan's Republican Party.

Japanese mass media has been changing

NHK has had the reputation of being pro-China, but this has been changing recently. For example, in 2019, they aired the one-million-people Hong Kong rally on their international broadcasting. But the program was blacked out in mainland China to prevent domestic viewing. The Beijing government forced the blackout of NHK's international broadcasting so people in China and Hong Kong would not be able to watch it.

This means that NHK is also reporting anti-Chinese coverage. This example illustrates that NHK is now very different from how it used to be. I believe it is going through a big change and should be more confident.

The Asahi Shimbun, *Tokyo Shimbun*, and *Chunichi Shimbun* newspapers have also been changing (*Tokyo Shimbun* and *Chunichi Shimbun* are run by the same group). This is a somewhat delicate matter because candidates aiming for political positions from the HRP may see these media as still having very different views from their own, but these newspapers are also going through a big change.

In April 2019, *the Asahi Shimbun* put out coverage of the Xinjiang Uyghur Autonomous Region. Given that their article was published one month after their on-site report was conducted, the Beijing government must have strictly censored their article.

Nevertheless, they were able to enter the region and report on the situation.

Looking back, when Happy Science stood against the Kodansha publishing company in 1991 over false stories of our organization in their magazine, *Friday*, *Asahi* supported us. It was the only newspaper that supported us. I do not know why, but they continually accused Kodansha of fraudulent activities, and I was surprised by their supportive stance towards us.

When we published *Allah's Great Warning* (currently out of publication) in the same year, showing our support to Muslim countries, *Asahi* was agreeable to us at that time as well. As I read their supportive articles, I thought they were unique. We both are unique, so I cannot say much of them.

There was another incident in 1995. From March of that year, we began our fight against the Aum Shinrikyo religious cult. We published a large book titled, *Operation to Exterminate Aum Shinrikyo*, and sold it throughout Japan. It was openly and repeatedly advertised. At that time, *Asahi* also wrote articles accusing the Aum Shinrikyo when all other newspaper companies shied away from writing about the cult. The other newspapers felt we were too bold. They observed for a week or so, to see who would win the case: the police or Aum Shinrikyo. They thought they would not write any articles if the police would lose, and they would only write articles if the police were likely to win.

In those circumstances, *Asahi* openly wrote critical articles. So, we applauded their reporters, saying, "You're brave. That's incredible," to which they replied, "Well, so are you." The Tokyo subway Sarin attack occurred after that, and we were both terrified to see what we were fighting against.

The Happiness Realization Party's policies go beyond Japanese standard ways of thinking

These things can happen, so I do not have a particular bias toward any media. It is fine to have different reports, and it is good that freedom of speech is guaranteed. Japan's national broadcasting and major newspapers may seem biased, but compared to the mass media of autocratic nations, they have sound ideas and voice their opinions. They are not completely controlled by the state. I believe that the media should be able to criticize the government as necessary.

The HRP is often classified as conservative. Yet, according to newspaper reports comparing each party's policies, we are listed both on the far left and on the far right, depending on the subject. They seemingly think that we say extreme things. Our policies probably sound very extreme by Japanese standards, but I want to say, "What are you saying? This is the Middle Way by the world standard."

As an individual, you should be confident in your life, work with confidence, and protect your family. To apply this idea on a national level, such healthy attitudes will naturally lead to the idea of protecting one's country on one's own. This is a natural way of thinking.

5

Issues that Need to be Reconsidered

Mr. Trump's criticism
On the Japan-U.S. Security Treaty is right

In June 2019, the G20 Summit was held in Osaka. Before and after coming to Japan, President Trump hinted at a possible revision of the Japan-U.S. alliance at the next possible opportunity. He stated, "We will fight World War III and protect Japan with our lives and with our treasure, but Japan can only watch it on a Sony television," criticizing the treaty as unfair.

To counter his criticism, Japanese newspapers all insisted, "Japan allows the U.S. troops to be stationed in Japan and provides financial support. The U.S. also benefits from it because they can launch an attack from their bases in Japan. So it is not a one-sided treaty."

I think Mr. Trump's honest feelings are right. According to the Japan-U.S. alliance, if Japan is attacked, be it Okinawa, Senkaku, or any other island, the U.S. must fight because it has the duty to protect Japan. However, when the U.S. comes under attack, Japan can look the other way. Naturally, Americans find that unfair.

Looking into Mr. Trump's true thoughts, we can see the next assertion the U.S. will make. He certainly wants to insist on a revision of Japan's Constitution. His true thoughts are: "Why not revise the constitution? Be smart! You say it was determined by MacArthur, but he is already gone from this world."

He means to say, "The sitting American president is telling Japan to revise its Constitution so hurry and do it; protect Japan on your own and reduce the burden put on America." This view precisely supports the idea of the HRP.

MacArthur is not a god. Even if he were, since I stand in a position of deciding whether to send him to hell, there is no need to admire him so much.

Our political opinions may now sound quite extreme, but this is due to the misguided ways of thinking that have long been implemented in Japanese education, news media, and other areas for over 70 years since the end of World War II. Look at the world from a completely clean slate; you will be able to see the world as we have pointed out.

The U.S.'s double standard toward Middle-East policies

Having said this, we do not always agree with the U.S. Regarding Iran, as written in my recent books, I have asked the U.S. to reconsider the immediate attack on Iran. I believe the U.S. needs to give more thought to the double standard they have.

What I mean by the double standard is this: When Islamic countries try to arm themselves with nuclear weapons, the international society fiercely accuses them and keeps their stock of enriched uranium under surveillance, whereas there was no argument when Israel silently and swiftly armed themselves with nuclear weapons. This shows that a double standard exists. From a neutral position, I feel there is something wrong with this.

It is very well for the country of Israel to exist. During World War II, the Nazis persecuted the Jewish people and six million Jews were killed in concentration camps. So it is good that they have a homeland to which they can return.

Jewish people began to return to the Holy Land in small groups from around the end of the 19th century. By the time World War II ended, some 700 thousand people had already settled there. With the approval of Western countries, Israel was founded in 1948. This was proper and should have been allowed.

However, since then, four wars have been fought in the Middle East, and Israel has increasingly expanded its military power during that time. From an objective perspective, I find this unfair.

The Jewish people entered a territory that was not their own and took a part of the land of Palestine so that they could establish their own state. Having taken up another's land, they should be more decent and behave better. When you move into a new apartment, you would certainly pay a visit to your neighbors and greet them to build a good relationship.

People in Israel had their country built in a land which did not belong to them, so I suggest they be more grateful and work to build a good relationship with the neighboring countries. Instead, they have equipped themselves with nuclear arms without people realizing it, and now possess hundreds of nuclear missiles and bombs. I think this has gone too far.

On the other hand, the U.S. and Israel accuse Iran of having a lot of enriched uranium and insist they must launch a preemptive attack. I feel the U.S. takes Israel's side too much.

Furthermore, there is the issue of the Golan Heights, which is effectively controlled by Israel. It was taken from Syria (Palestinians) in the Six-Day War. Palestinians inherently regard the Golan Heights as their territory, though it is now occupied by Israel.

Recently, Israeli Prime Minister Netanyahu named a settlement in the Golan Heights area Trump Heights, an expression of Israeli gratitude to him. This was rather a cunning tactic. Now that it has been named the Trump Heights, if it were attacked, the U.S. would feel as if it was being attacked and they would have to dispatch their Fifth Fleet. In this sense, Prime Minister Netanyahu came up with a clever idea.

I wish Mr. Trump would have declined the offer. It should have been renamed Netanyahu Heights, instead of Trump Heights, then it would be possible for the surrounding Arab countries to attack it. It seems Mr. Trump has been skillfully taken in.

6

A New Philosophy and
The World's Future Design
That Japan Must Advocate

The Truth about God of Christianity and Allah of Islam

There certainly is a double standard, and the underlying idea is this: Some Christians consider Muslim countries as nations of the Devil, illustrated by the hardline stance of former U.S. National Security Adviser John Bolton. They probably believe that Islamic teachings are essentially those of the Devil. On the other hand, there are also people in Muslim countries who see the U.S. as demonic. Due to this mutual distrust, American hardliners say that there is no option but to settle the problem by force.

But there is a limit to how much any political negotiation or military power can do to solve this issue. I believe it is time for religion to step in and mediate the problem between the two sides. The time has come sooner than I expected.

At the starting point of Christianity, Jesus had the Father in Heaven who was guiding him. Whenever Jesus cured illnesses, gave a sermon in front of thousands of people, or performed various miracles, the Father in Heaven was always guiding him. This is clearly written in the New Testament.

What is the relation between this Father in Heaven and the being that Prophet Muhammad called Allah (the Arabic word for God) 600 years later? No one has answered it, so now I dare say: The Heavenly Father that Jesus called upon and Allah that Prophet Muhammad called upon were the same Being.

Therefore, Christianity and Islam have the same root; they believe in the same God. I want them to stop fighting each other, as they believe in the same God.

A further religious explanation would be necessary to understand this Truth,* but their fighting will get them nowhere, so I want them to stop fighting. I believe only Japan, an Eastern country, can be the mediator.

The Truth about the God of Judaism

Israel is also a country with its own unique tradition and history; it has many important teachings that are described in the Old Testament and are worth studying, so it is better to preserve

---

*TF: Refer to *The Laws of the Sun, The Golden Laws* and *The Nine Dimensions*. See page 253.

Israel as well. However, it now shows some traits of an aggressor nation, so I believe we must put a stop to this tendency and tell them to behave properly.

Israel had not existed for 1,900 years. I have to say that a god who had neglected his people for such a long time cannot be the All-Knowing, Almighty God.

There certainly were gods who had guided Israel in the past, but now most of them are gone. Only a certain number of ethnic gods have remained and others have already dispersed. It is not right to forcibly spread the teachings of such ethnic gods to the entire world. While it is right for Israelis to strive to protect their own country, they should stop at that level. It is wrong to desire to govern the whole of the Islamic world by attacking other nations with nuclear weapons. I oppose this idea.

I do not agree with all of Mr. Trump's ideas. I voice my opinion based on what is right.

Be confident in spreading the philosophy
That will help solve conflicts around the world

My philosophy will help create a kingdom of the soul
That was given by God or Buddha,
In the heart of each person.

It will also help you make
Your home and place of work shine forth,
And enrich your country.
As this philosophy extends farther, beyond national borders,
It will contribute to creating order and harmony in the world
To achieve world justice.
Such work is lying ahead of us.

We must be confident in our lives.
Be more confident in your life.
Only Happy Science is now conveying
The teachings of the Ultimate God of this Earth.

Please spread these teachings all over Japan and the world.
I ask this of you;
For this effort will be salvation for the world.
Happy Science teachings will be able to overcome problems
That neither Islam nor Christianity can solve,
And save the world.

I ask you to be stronger,
Develop your power,
Achieve further success,
And speak up more.

Go beyond national borders,
And expand your power to the world.
I ask all of you from my heart.

MESSAGE FROM EL CANTARE, GOD OF THE EARTH

Now, I tell you this.

"Lord God" in Christianity,

"Elohim" in Judaism,

"Allah" in Islam,

"Shangdi," or the emperor in heaven,

Referred to by Confucius of China,

And "Ame-no-Mioya-Gami"[*] in Japanese Shinto,

The one above the central god

Ame-no-Minakanushi-no-Kami

Whose profile remains unknown,

Are all the same, single Being.

Religions differ in their ways of thinking

Due to differences in ethnicity and culture.

---

[*] TF: Ame-no-Mioya-Gami is the creator god who appears in an ancient Japanese text called "Hotsuma Tsutae," a document that is said to be older than the Japanese mythic texts, "Kojiki" and "Nihon Shoki."

However, there is only one origin;

People are all friends

Undergoing soul training together on earth

As they refine their souls in various ways.

I created the system of reincarnation,

So that people can go beyond the barrier of ethnic groups.

Although you may be Japanese today,

You may have been European, Chinese, Korean, or another

In your past lives, or vice versa.

By going through such soul experiences,

Perhaps experiencing past lives as both male and female,

You are trying to broaden your capacity

To understand each other.

I was born in this land of Japan

To teach the last, the final, and all Laws.

I will reveal everything I know.

I say unto you.

Humankind must learn the Words of the True God,

Overcome their differences, reconcile and harmonize,

And strive to evolve and develop.

These are the Words of El Cantare, God of the Earth.

You shall not forget this ever again.

Engrave this into your heart.

Humankind is one.

From now on,

Believe in the existence of God

Who surpasses worldly conflicts

And, under God,

Choose to continue with the world

That upholds freedom and democracy.

What North Korea needs is faith.

What China needs is faith, too.

What India needs is God above various gods.

What the Islamic nations need is to learn who Allah is.

I love and accept humankind beyond their differences.

Through believing,

Learn what love is.

This is my message.

Chapter FIVE

A SAVIOR'S WISH

Awakening to the Life of Service to the World

Lecture given on April 29, 2019
at Special Lecture Hall, Happy Science, Tokyo, Japan

1

The Awareness
That Your True Self is a Soul

This chapter deals with a difficult theme, and I believe it is now necessary to organize our thoughts. To begin with, let us return to the starting point: "What is a Savior?" To answer this question, we need to consider once again the nature of this world on earth.

This world is an extremely challenging place for a Savior and other higher beings, including angels working under the Savior, to be born in a human body. The reason for this is because, in this world, most parts of the Truth are concealed. Therefore, the majority of people on earth do not know about the truth.

For example, people may believe that they know a lot about themselves, but how many people actually know that a soul resides in their physical body and is in control of it? I suppose only a very few people are truly aware of this.

Among religious believers, some may have such knowledge. However, are they truly aware, as they lead their everyday physical lives, that their true self is a soul residing in their physical body? How many of them are deeply awakened to the fact as they live that it is their soul that is using their physical body to gain various experiences and carry out work on earth? I am afraid the number of such people is extremely few.

If we consider those who clearly grasped this truth, Socrates of ancient times most certainly did. That is why he was not afraid to face death when he drank a cup of hemlock poison. He placed the utmost importance on leaving behind what his immortal soul achieved in his life. Individuals such as Socrates have existed in history, but they are rare.

Jesus Christ is another example. The description of Jesus' death differs in each Gospel. But if, as described in some Gospels (Matthew and Mark), Jesus had cried out on the cross, "My God, My God, why have you forsaken me?" it would, unfortunately, mean that Jesus was a mere physical being bound to this earthly world, someone who understood his purpose as just to survive on earth.

The truth is different, however, according to Happy Science's spiritual research. Jesus, in fact, knew the time had come for his death and called out on the cross, "Elijah, Elijah, Raphael, Raphael, come take me away." But some Gospels have interpreted his words to mean, "My God, My God, why have you forsaken me?" and there are people who actually believe this. It is truly unfortunate. These Gospels were written based on the writers' assumptions of how they would personally feel. If this was what Jesus had truly meant, it would mean that Jesus lacked the true awareness of being a Savior. Moreover, this description being retained in the Bible until now has shown the level of faith of the churches that have preserved it.

When Jesus entered Jerusalem, he knew his time had come to leave this world. So, he willingly went to be crucified. It was to fulfill prophecies that had been foretold 1,000 years earlier that we can read in the Old Testament (Books of Isaiah and Zechariah). We can understand the prophecies as follows: A Messiah will be born, who will later enter into Jerusalem on a donkey while crowds are shouting, "Hosanna [save us]"; the Son of David will then be crucified and finally ascend to heaven. Jesus acted in accordance with what the prophecies had foretold to make it come true. He chose that path because he believed in the prophecies and because he had actually been told to do so by the heavenly world.

Many of his disciples, however, were caught up with worldly matters and attempted to escape. They pleaded with Jesus to escape rather than remain and be caught and crucified. The Apostle Peter denied knowing Jesus three times when accused of being one of his followers, though this man who had forsaken Jesus in this way would later go on to become the first Pope.

There was such a huge difference in awareness between master and disciples. It is only natural that disciples with this level of awareness had many misunderstandings and some elements were beyond their comprehension when writing the Gospels.

2

The Faith to Become One
With God or Buddha

✧   ✧   ✧

The true meaning of Shinran's teaching

In the case of Shinran (1173 - 1262), the founder of True Pure Land Buddhism, many of his disciples also misunderstood his teaching that "Even people who have committed evil can be saved."

The idea that "evil people are the ones who can be saved" was actually not Shinran's original teaching, but that of his teacher Honen (1133 - 1212). Shinran himself had broken some precepts and failed to undergo strict spiritual discipline as a monk. He was deeply aware of his sins, and this caused him to refer to himself as someone who had committed evil. On the other hand, Honen, the original teacher, was purely monastic and respected by others; he was studious and abided by the precepts without breaking any vows until he died in his 70s. He was the one who first said that evil people are the ones who can be saved, though it is now more commonly believed that Shinran first taught it and his disciple Yuien had written it down in text. This notion triggers great misunderstanding depending on how it is interpreted.

This world is filled with opportunity for salvation for those who know the true meaning of Buddha's or Amitabha Buddha's great power of salvation and can become one with its Light. But those who do not believe in Amitabha Buddha's power of salvation can only see this world as a completely dark place. That is why Shinran taught that Amitabha Buddha's Light extends to this earthly world saying, "Look at the Light and seek salvation, then you can become one with Amitabha Buddha."

There are very few people who can grasp the true meaning of this teaching. It teaches that if one attains the deepest levels of faith, one will experience for themselves the truth: "Faith is salvation." Very few can understand this idea. As time has passed, some have even interpreted it as a simplistic idea that committing evil is the way to salvation.

Shinran, although a monk, acted against Buddhist precepts and led a "half secular half sacred" life. That is why he deeply reflected on his thoughts and deeds, and profoundly regretted his sins. He said, "I could choose a different path of Buddhist discipline to find salvation, but I would certainly not be able to be saved that way. So I will rely on the teaching of 'Namo Amitabha Buddha' and follow Honen faithfully even if I were to be deceived and led to hell. I am prepared to face any outcome." What he wanted to teach most was the importance of having such deep devotion.

Shinran disowned his eldest son
For distorting his teaching

Shinran sought to spread his teaching in the eastern regions of Japan when there were no convenient modes of transportation and communication, so he sent his eldest son Zenran there to do missionary work. Zenran, however, distorted his father's teaching in order to expand the number of followers. Rather than fully explaining the essence of Shinran's teaching, he taught that with more evil deeds, one could reach salvation faster. He spread this idea to increase the number of followers.

Having learned of the misleading idea Zenran was spreading, Shinran in his final years disowned his eldest son, going so far as to sever all ties between father and son. Shinran, who taught that evil people are the ones who can be saved, went this far. Why was it? It was because Zenran's idea was different from the original teaching.

In the modern context, the essence of this teaching can be explained in the following way: "If several patients in critical condition were brought in to a hospital emergency room by ambulance at the same time, doctors would naturally begin treating the most urgent and critically ill patients first. Patients in less need of emergency care would be treated later. That would accord with the Will of Buddha." If taken to extremes, however, it would lead to the idea that the more sins one commits, the more one will be saved. This would mean that a person who murdered three people would be more quickly saved than a person who killed one; salvation would be even quicker for a person who killed 10.

This logic is obviously flawed. Where lies the mistake? To cite Shinran's words, it would be: "Here's an antidote, so drink all the poison you like—words like that should never be said." One should never encourage others to drink poison just because there is an effective antidote for it. Think about the children, and you will understand that Shinran was right. However, sometimes people cannot understand the subtle difference. Herein lies the difficult aspect of salvation in this world.

In the world of faith, if you want to become one with the Being called God or Buddha, you must take a truly great leap from this world to reach the far-distant heavenly world. However, people in this world are apt to try to bring God or Buddha down to their earthly level and speak of His existence as if on equal footing. This is clearly shown in the example cited above.

3
Efforts Required of a Savior

✧　✧　✧

Even a Savior must be humble

When it comes to salvation, the focus must ultimately be on saving souls in this world. Depending on the era, different ordeals may befall humankind. Sometimes, wars will occur; among those who have been called a Savior, some were ethnic gods and they may have worked hard to save their own particular ethnic groups. There could have been wars between ethnic gods. Nevertheless, it is imperative that "what was right" is explored beyond life and death in this world, and the prime intention or aim of Saviors must always be to establish on earth what is held as right in the Real World. This point should never be neglected.

To be a Savior in this world, one must have appropriate self-awareness, power, courage, a strong will to take action, and words of teaching. This person would inevitably have a power of great influence in this world and a worldly power that would resemble other secular authorities. For this reason, it is very difficult to tell who is a Savior, and who is under the power of the devils that try to rule over the earthly world. In many cases, the truth cannot be known until an era has passed.

What is it that we must humbly reflect upon at such times? It is the fact that even for Light of Great Angels or Grand Guiding Spirits, once they dwell in a physical body, it is impossible to know everything about the Real World, so they can only reveal part of its secrets. They need to be well aware that only a fragment of the Truth is sent down to them. They also need to know that they are subject to the constraints of a specific era. It is undeniable that their teachings are largely influenced by the way of life of that age.

For this reason, even a Savior must remain humble in this world. Once in the vessel of a human body, one must make efforts, accumulate spiritual discipline, and pursue the spiritual Path, in order to deepen one's awareness as a child of Light.

Embodying the mercy of God or Buddha

The first challenge one encounters when aspiring to achieve greatness in this world is that one's efforts tend to become unwittingly selfish, around the end of adolescence. Being born as a human with an individual character, everyone is more or less expected to achieve their goals in life. Everyone is born and raised in different kinds of environments and has a certain physical body and talents inherited from their parents. They are born in a specific place and country, and find an occupation. Under these conditions, there are certain spiritual disciplines that one needs to undergo to become awakened. However, these disciplines of self-awakening, which can appear to be efforts for self-actualization, are not meant for living an easier life in this world.

Becoming awakened means that you become deeply aware that you are here to illuminate the world; you are Light itself and have a mission to save people who are suffering in the darkness. At the same time, you should develop your abilities and make them your power to accomplish more work.

Therefore, even if one were to hold a position of leadership by birth, bloodline, or appointed status, one cannot be called a true Savior if, in simple words, one has no virtue, is hated by others, and is not loved in the truest sense. What is considered "love" in this world certainly includes "love that merely takes", so love can often be misunderstood. But the Love of God or Buddha will ultimately lead to mercy; it is not the mutual love of equals, but the love that only gives. One must embody this mercy in some way. The embodiment of mercy must manifest in various forms of virtue. We need to know this.

To lead eight billion people in the world

A large number of people are now living in this world. This means that there are many different ways of life and many different ways of thinking. To be able to save the souls of these many diverse people, it is necessary to have the capacity to understand them. It is not possible to deal with all the challenges in this lifetime just based on accomplishments of past lives from thousands of years ago. The current population on Earth is nearing eight billion, a massive and unprecedented number of people. To guide such a great number of people, different kinds of study will obviously be required in this lifetime.

Those who are referred to as a Savior, tathagata, archangel or angel, will often appear in this world as geniuses in various fields. A genius would be described as a person who is highly capable without much learning, innately highly talented, a quick learner compared to others, or early to find personal talent and bring it to full blossom. Some people are regarded to be geniuses as a result of their achievements. However, in a world with such a large population, if one has a mission to greatly influence people and lead them in a certain direction, one must persevere in their efforts continuously. One must keep making efforts to study the various problems of this world and seek to find solutions to them.

In modern society, one cannot save people solely based on spiritual inspiration. To develop solutions to the many problems of this world, one must make efforts, study things, and understand the minds of many people. These efforts must not be pretense or a performance but must truly affect people's hearts.

We must not forget the essential truth

Occasionally, artists can have great influence over a large number of people. There is certainly no problem if their influence conveys the true meaning of love, helps people overcome their suffering, or becomes a guidepost to happiness. However, sometimes an artist's work becomes popular in this world with the opposite effect. Someone can gain popularity or be given a high status even though their work is detrimental to the world. This is the trend of this world and it sometimes goes in the wrong direction.

At such times, it is important to remember the essential truth. Earlier I said that people on earth tend to forget that a soul inhabits their physical body, but that is not all they forget. The majority of people do not even understand the simple truth that human souls essentially belong to the spirit world and are born as infants in this world to live and grow old. They do not even understand what happens after death.

Mainstream Christianity denies the idea of reincarnation. Many Buddhists, especially those who tend to misunderstand its teachings, interpret Buddhism as closer to materialism. Some professors at Buddhist universities in Japan even teach that everything ends with death and humans just turn into ashes. These people probably think that it makes no difference whether ashes are scattered in the ocean or under a tree, or that there is no point in conducting memorial services for the deceased. It is sad to reach such a conclusion after studying Buddhism.

There are also Buddhists who believe that since Shakyamuni Buddha entered Nirvana in the heavenly world after having attained enlightenment through spiritual discipline 2,500 years ago, he will never return to this world or have any ties with it; he will be gone forever as if his soul has vanished. It seems that their understanding of enlightenment is based on an extremely self-righteous idea that has nothing to do with saving people.

The truth, however, is that a soul that has returned to its original abode in the higher realm of the spirit world will continuously work to save people who are lost. That is its true intention. This shows that, as time passes, religious doctrines by humans have become largely influenced by their minds and thoughts.

Virtue will be lost if you are not in tune with heaven

In Japan, people used to worship the Emperor as a living god, especially after the Meiji Restoration (1868). This belief has often been practiced in Japan since ancient times. I suppose some countries have had similar ideas in their past, in which people often believed that kings served the role of gods. It is certainly true that a great soul sometimes inhabits the body of someone in a ruling position, but still, I believe that the person should always remain humble, have strong self-control, and be filled with merciful love toward people.

Japan will soon experience the transition from the Heisei Period to the Reiwa Period (at the time of the lecture). People are probably discussing it in many ways. Some may be simply celebrating the continuation of the Japanese Imperial Household. However, I am afraid that at present, it is in a very precarious situation. It seems that the Emperor himself is not sure of the meaning of being an Emperor, and neither are the politicians, the Diet, nor the Japanese people who sustain the system. The Emperor seems to project the image of a historical absolute monarch, and at the same time, is a symbolic figure who has no real power. It seems that the politicians elected by the people have all the real power. In this sense, the footing of the Japanese Imperial Household is extremely fragile and in danger.

For this reason, should the Imperial Family lose virtue in the future, they might lose the support of the people, and there would be an extremely strong possibility that a new dictator could emerge. They need to understand that the Imperial Household has a long lineage from ancient Japanese gods, and that they are responsible for performing Shinto religious rituals. Unless they understand this, or sincerely pray for the peace of this nation, they will not be able to understand the meaning of their very existence or convey it to the people.

The current trend appears to be similar to the immediate postwar days; the Emperor's role is being redefined to human status. That is what I perceive. I have the impression that more people in the Imperial Family would not hesitate to show regular human behavior, having the desire to enjoy freedom and pleasures just like common people do. If this is due to the deterioration of the souls inhabiting the physical bodies of Imperial Family members, their future will truly be harsh.

I wish they would strive to awaken more deeply to their spiritual mission and increase their power of virtue. I also hope they will stay above politics, where people unite or separate based on interests. If the Imperial Family continues to remain the target of abuse by weekly magazines, their future cannot be fully guaranteed. Regardless of the regulations in the Constitution of Japan, I believe that they must be in tune with God or Buddha in wishing for the happiness of the people. That is my message for them now.

4

The Mission of a Savior

✧　　✧　　✧

Desires to achieve earthly self-realization
Can easily become food for devils

Given this background, Happy Science, a religion, is now emerging in Japan. The mission of Happy Science is not limited to protecting Japan and bringing it prosperity. Although originating in Japan, Happy Science carries out the work of teaching the Will of God, the Source, so that the differences of various races and religions, which had separated into various parts of the world, will not become seeds of conflict. I am trying to give teachings that govern the entire Earth.

I am sure that as we proceed, there will be many difficulties that block our way. I do not know how far we can go, but we must know that this world contains a mixture of good and evil. We must also know that those with selfish desires are constantly receiving invitations from the evil empire of hell, which is formed by devils.

There will be no problem if your desire to achieve your goals expands for a sacred purpose, but if your self-realization is confined to this world and is focused on gaining a benefit for yourself, those desires will serve as food for devils. We must know this.

Even among highly talented people, there are probably many who will receive an invitation from devils. Even if a true religion strives to awaken them to the Truth, many may be tempted away by the devils' invitations on their way to awakening. That is because accepting the devils' invitations will often mean having luxury, fame, or wealth in this world.

Distinguishing good from evil and
Leading people in the right direction

It is difficult to restrain power when one has it. It is also very difficult to control supernatural ability rationally. Again, it is difficult to use political and financial powers in a good direction when one has them. For example, in a company, it is very difficult for those in superior positions to be aware of their great influence on the lives of many employees working there. While there is this difficulty in leading others, we are nevertheless born into this temporary world and continue our spiritual discipline before we return to the Real World. This is the reality that everyone—from a Savior to those who have come under the devils' rule—cannot escape.

In the process, fights may occur. Battles between light and darkness may also arise. Deciding what is light and what is darkness, or what is good and what is evil in the same age—this is the power of a Savior. It is also the wish of a Savior. Indicating the true direction that people should move forward in, leading them to stop doing evil and to choose goodness, opening the way to the next life—this is the mission of a Savior. In the field of politics, it can also appear as creating a barrier to prevent hell from forming on earth. This is also important.

5

Live This Life to the Fullest
As a Tool of God or Buddha

Everything is for God

Powers that one has gained in this world, the desire to win over others that arises from a competitive nature, the desire for fame, and various other desires—these elements will cause talented people to fall from grace. Therefore, no matter how your position changes in the future, in order to protect what must be protected and to be truly of service to God, it is essential to perceive that everything is for God.

It goes without saying that even a Savior is only a tool of God in this world. While a Savior is born into this world to fulfill God's purpose, there is no doubt that they will awaken to their full original consciousness after returning to the other world.

God's words are everything

Now that we are living in a very difficult period when the world has so many problems and supports a huge population, we need to make tremendous efforts to prevent hell from forming on earth. At the same time, it is also true that we have entered the age when it is extremely difficult to teach so many people about heaven and hell and the ideal world that God wishes to create.

The advancement of the machine civilization will not be hampered by the belief in materialism; maybe it will bring more benefits. If life was limited only to this world, it would be preferable for life on earth to be easier and more comfortable, so the more the world becomes convenient, the better it would be. Such a world would produce more people without a sense of guilt even if they killed someone. Everything, including good and evil, could be determined by artificial intelligence (AI), unlike what I said earlier, and a time may come when people start to destroy others at the order of AI.

However, no matter what kind of age may come, and even if machines are invented to calculate much faster than humans and store much more knowledge and information, AI will never surpass the Wisdom of God. Therefore, in the end, it is essential to be aware that God's words are everything.

Live out your life for others and the world

We are living in such a difficult time and there are many important points to teach. Each person has much work to do and, as they carry out their specialized jobs, some may be deluded by the desire for power or fame, and hide themselves within a shell of self-preservation. There will be no end; such people will keep on appearing.

Therefore, purify your mind and make it clear. Always return to the starting point and be aware that you should live out your life for others and the world; that is the hundred years of life given to you. This is important. And, to keep this attitude in your life, you must always stay awakened to spirituality.

Never forget spirituality. This world is not everything, nor is an academic background, any earthly power, the company one works for, or material possessions. Physical beauty does not matter. These are not important. What is truly important is how deeply you are connected to God or Buddha, whether you are one with Him. It is essential to live this life to the fullest as a tool of God or Buddha.

A Savior is born on earth to this end. Once you hear the Savior's command, come join them and work together. That is important.

If left as it is, this earthly world will become more advantageous for the devils to gain power. With the increase in population, the number of people who believe that this world is all that exists has also increased.

The time is now when we must gain much greater power.

Awakened ones must come forward in great numbers.

People with a spiritual disposition must be careful not to misuse their spiritual ability as they live.

In this chapter, I have spoken on a Savior's wish. I sincerely hope that, as you are fully aware of the difficulties of living in the modern age, you will strictly control yourself and keep moving forward.

Abandon,
If You Want to Protect

To enter the world of Light of Angels,

"Protecting" alone is not enough;

"Abandoning" is also critical.

It is important to cast away all things

Other than what is truly valuable.

Those who have failed to do this

Cannot enter the world of angels.

What you must abandon is worldly attachment.

Many things seem valuable

From an earthly perspective,

But if you consider life after death,

You will realize that

You should cast all these things away.

I have repeatedly taught that

When you die,

All you can take with you to the other world

Is your mind.

But the mind can include both good and evil thoughts,

And depending on what kind of mind

You take with you,

Your destination will differ, either heaven or hell.

Therefore, the mind is not the ultimate thing.

To advance this teaching a step further,

We need the right faith.

The true teaching would be:

"Take the right faith with you

When you return to the other world."

The mind itself is not sufficient;

You must have the right faith.

As long as you have the right faith,

You will need nothing more.

Everything else will eventually vanish from this world,

And you cannot take any of it with you.

There is no choice but to abandon all in the end.

While "protecting" is one way of thinking,

There is another idea: "Abandoning."

Recently I have often used the expression,

"Die for the Truth."

It means being ready to abandon

All that is not of true value.

To die for the Truth means

Being willing to even abandon this life on earth.

I have such determination.

Our life in this world is not so long,

So what matters is

Continuously sowing many seeds of Truth

For people who will come hundreds

Or even thousands of years from now.

My mission is not limited to bringing happiness

To people who are living now.

I must continue to sow the seeds of Truth,

Even if they do not sprout right away,

To bring happiness to the people of the future,

Who will come hundreds

And even thousands of years from now.

The seeds that are sown now will eventually lose life,

But they will bear fruits,

Which, in time, will produce a harvest

That is hundreds or thousands times greater.

It may not happen until much later in the distant future,

But that is where my eyes are looking.

You can serve as the soil to grow those seeds,

To save many people in the distant future.

Even if a seed is sown,

It cannot sprout without good soil.

I want you to be the "good soil."

"Protecting" is important.

But "abandoning" is also important.

And curiously,

Sometimes "protecting" is the same as "abandoning."

Similar to a Zen koan,

I would say, "Abandon, if you want to protect."

Abandoning is surprisingly important.

What do you throw away?

And what is it that is left in the end?

Ask yourself these questions.

I, too, work in this manner.

Chapter SIX

THE POWER TO MAKE MIRACLES

*Opening Your Future with a Transparent Mind,
the Practice of Love, and Prayer*

Lecture given on December 11, 2018
at Makuhari Messe International Exhibition Hall, Chiba, Japan

1

The Power to Draw the Future to the Present

My primary goal:
Giving 3,000 lectures and publishing 2,500 books

The lecture on which this chapter is based was given at the end of 2018; it marked my 151st lecture for that year and the 2,848th lecture in total. My primary goal has been to give 3,000 lectures, and I feel I should push myself to achieve it in 2019. In terms of books, my goal is to achieve 2,500 publications. I feel I am close to reaching these initial goals. (Note: Okawa's publications exceeded 2,500 as of January 2019, and 2,600 as of December 2019.)

When I started Happy Science, a large Japanese religious group called *Seicho-no-Ie* had already existed. Its founder, Masaharu Taniguchi, gave about 3,000 lectures during the 55-years from the time he founded his religious group until he died at the age of 91. So I set 3,000 lectures as an initial goal for myself, and I see now that I will likely achieve it in about 33 years.

I am not saying I am doing better than he did; it is not about the quality of each lecture. I just continued my efforts to make some progress, using every chance I got. There were certainly times I faced difficulties I was not sure I could overcome, but when I did manage to get over them, I was very happy.

Witnessing of many UFOs after my lecture, "The Opening of the Space Age"

In the summer of 2018, I gave a public lecture, "The Opening of the Space Age."* I felt hesitant to speak about this because members of the mass media were also in attendance at the invitation of Happy Science Public Relations Division, and I thought it was a little too early in Japan.

I think more than 100 people from the mass media attended my lecture at Makuhari Messe. I certainly am grateful that they attend my lecture, but it makes it difficult for me to speak because there is a large gap between the awareness of our ardent, long-time believers and the perspective of other people outside our organization.

Then, after I gave the lecture on the coming space age that summer, suddenly we could shoot many pictures and videos of UFOs, and it was found that UFOs had been appearing to help promote our activities.

---

* TF: Refer to Chapter Four of *The Laws of Bronze* (New York: IRH Press, 2019).

In the fall of the same year, our animated film, *The Laws of the Universe – Part I* was released in theaters, and it became our first hit production in 15 years (since *The Golden Laws*, released in 2003). It was also favorably received in the United States, so I had high expectations for it.

Perceiving the future as if it happens in the present

During the year 2018, I planned out our successive movie projects, which would extend to 2025. This is how I usually work; I plan far out into the future to make sure the project will ultimately be a success.

The movie project also gave me opportunities to compose music. Two of the songs I wrote were introduced in the welcome program at the opening of the lecture covered in this chapter. Initially, I meant to show the music video for entertainment before my lectures; I never imagined I would be creating much music for movies. But the number of songs I wrote has now increased to the point that I worry that people might mistake songwriting as my main job. I think I have released about 30 songs or so, but I have actually composed over 80 songs.[*] I have already composed music which will be used years later. This number is surprising even for me, but since this lecture is about miracles, I think it is OK.

I am able to experience the future. I can perceive the future—what happens next year, the year after that, five years from now, or even 10 years—as if it is happening right now. I focus my mind on the types of work I will be doing at a particular time in the future, and detailed images of that time will then form inside my mind in the present as if being drawn. I live based on such a perspective of life.

---

*TF: As of January 2019, Okawa has written and composed over 100 songs.

2

Continuous Work Based on Miracles

✧   ✧   ✧

Without miracles, no founding of Happy Science
Nor 30-plus years of missionary activities

Regarding "the Power to Make Miracles," I myself have
experienced a succession of miracles, so for me, it is unbelievable
for miracles *not* to happen. Honestly speaking, my work has been
based on miracles. Without miracles, the founding of Happy
Science and the more than 30 years of missionary activities would
not have been possible.

Well over 10,000 people came to this lecture at Makuhari
Messe, and it was broadcast to about 3,500 locations around
the world, including locations in different time zones. When it
comes to religion in Japan, numbers are often downplayed when
reported, so some people may believe that the people gathering
at a particular event represent the entire membership. The truth
is that Happy Science has more than 30,000 believers just in
Nepal, the birthplace of Shakyamuni Buddha; we also have a
large, stupa-style local temple there. We also have hundreds of
thousands of believers in India. Our global membership has
grown so large that we cannot keep up with our operations. I am

afraid our overseas members are enduring a low level of service. Even so, their activities are supported by the precious donations from the Japanese members. Thanks to their support, we are able to carry out various activities.

My books are printed worldwide in hundreds of millions

Recently, I was able to give a lecture in Germany, and I addressed the audience with all the countries of the EU in mind.[*] Returning from Germany, I was convinced that Japan is indeed an advanced nation. In terms of GDP, Germany probably comes just after Japan, but when I actually visited there, I found that in many areas Japan is much more advanced. It is somewhat unfortunate that Japanese people fail to see how advanced a country they live in. I feel that there is yet an even greater gap in development between Japan and other countries besides Germany. Although Japanese people tend to undervalue themselves, I believe Japan has now succeeded in creating something to be proud of.

The first time I gave a lecture in the International Hall at Makuhari Messe was in 1990. Since then I have given many more in the 28 years that have passed. Many people have supported Happy Science and carried out various activities in Japan and all

---

[*] TF: This lecture is compiled in Part One, Chapter One of *Love for the Future* (New York: IRH Press, 2019).

over the world. I am happy to see that my teachings are spreading all around the world thanks to the efforts of our many supporters.

My books are published not only in Japanese but are also translated into 31 foreign languages. To be honest, the total number of books in print is not countable anymore; it is estimated to be in the hundreds of millions. The number of people who have heard my lectures is also hard to count because, in some developing countries, screenings of my recorded lectures are shown in many locations. It is almost impossible to count the exact number—most probably some 500 million to a billion people.

We also produce many movies. In addition to screenings in movie theaters, we also tour different areas overseas and show them in many locations. I suppose the total viewership of our movies has also reached a level that is impossible to tell. Most of these overseas activities are possible thanks to the strong support of our Japanese members, and I am very grateful for this.

Overcoming people's fixed idea of "We can't"

When I first started using Makuhari Messe as a lecture venue 28 years ago, I began by using the Event Hall, a smaller lecture hall with a capacity of around 7,000 people. The acoustics were good, so it was easy for me to give a lecture there. On the other hand, the International Exhibition Hall, which was used for this lecture, was not designed for speech presentations. So when we first considered holding lectures there, it was quite difficult to determine whether it would really be possible.

People around me worried that the pillars would obstruct the audience's view, that my voice would not reach the back, that my voice would echo off the walls and get jumbled, that the air-conditioning would not work well, or that there would not be enough restrooms, and so on. Many reasons came up why it would not work, but I somehow overcame these difficulties using wisdom and finally managed to make it work.

At the time, I would never have imagined that 28 years later I would be broadcasting from that site by satellite to about 3,500 other locations around the world. Another thing that has surprised me is our members' continued participation. I did not expect so many people would still be so involved even after they reach my current age. I am very grateful. Those once-vibrant youth may have changed after all these years, but it makes me very happy to see them continuously shining.

The magic of changing yourself
While staying young at heart

While this may not qualify as a miracle, it also seems that I have not been aging either. Somehow, I am not getting older. Retirement age in Japan is usually set around 60, and the government is now trying to extend this to around 65. I personally feel like, "Retire at 60? Why would someone retire so young?"

Sometimes, when I go shopping with my daughter, people mistakenly think that I am her co-worker. It secretly makes me happy. It may not be a good thing for my daughter, but when people ask us, "Are you colleagues or friends?" I just chuckle.

Magic is not just about turning something into gold. Keep on changing yourself while staying young at heart—this is also a form of magic.

When I would give a lecture at the International Exhibition Hall as a young man, I was full of energy and gave it my all; my voice would echo tremendously. As a result, people sometimes could not make out what I said. Now, however, I can deliver a lecture quite comfortably in front of an audience of 14,000. In fact, I would like to have an even larger audience. I wish I were able to view the people listening to my lecture around the world at the same time, so I could get feedback on their reactions too. This may become a reality in the near future.

3

Many More Miracles are Certain to Occur

Happy Science movies make miracles happen

With such an introduction, let me now focus on this chapter's topic, miracles. While already many miracles have happened till now, I want to make even more of them happen in the coming years.

One way is through movies. *The Last White Witch* was released in February 2019 (Executive Producer and original story by Ryuho Okawa). I have enchanted this movie. The movie itself and its theme song contain a magic spell, so those who see this movie will be enchanted and miracles will occur. This was the plan for the first part of 2019.

Another movie came out in October 2019 titled *Immortal Hero* (Executive Producer and original story by Ryuho Okawa). This film is based on an incident that happened to me about 15 years ago (2004). Some parts were altered for the movie adaptation, but 80 percent of it is accurately depicted. It is a visual account of the miraculous experience I had 15 years ago.

I heard that the movie director prayed every morning so that those who would see it would be healed of their illnesses. He prayed for this as he filmed. That was his first prayer. His second prayer was to wish that his *ikiryo* (the combination of one's strong thoughts and their guardian spirit) would not go and bother me. Apparently, he prayed for these two things early in the morning before filming every day. So much prayer has gone into this movie that I expect that there would be many miracles of recovering illness after its release.

Countless miracles have been happening At Happy Science

At Happy Science, there have already been hundreds to thousands of reports of illnesses being healed. We do not trouble ourselves to count them specifically since there are so many, but I believe many miracles are happening nationwide and around the world.

Sometimes you can read or watch these stories in our monthly magazines or other media. I learn about these miracles through such media, just like you all do. This may sound odd but since these miracles are common occurrences, they are not reported to me. I suppose there are so many miracles to report.

One rare example happened in December 2017, when Aide

to Master & CEO Shio Okawa and actress Yoshiko Sengen held a Christmas event based on the picture book, *Panda Roonda* (available at Happy Science local branches and temples) at Tokyo Shoshinkan. Many children took part in the event where they enjoyed a picture-story show along with singing and dancing. During the event, gold powder fell from above. When the same performance was screened later at different venues, a lot of gold powder came down again. We have collected records of these incidents.

Surprisingly, those gold particles appear just for a reading event of a picture book for children. This would be shocking news to physicists today, but there is no denying that this happened. The falling particles are clearly visible, but of course, their amount is not enough to make you rich; they appear as powder and cannot be gathered up to be exchanged for money.

Children have pure hearts, so I suppose many angels come when there is an event for children, such as a reading of picture books or other presentations. I believe the gold powder phenomenon happens as proof of this truth. This type of occurrence actually has taken place since the early days of Happy Science; when we held an event especially for children, such phenomena seemed to happen more often.

I think similar phenomena are likely to take place around the world, so please have your smartphones ready to record them. It is great that gold powder appears but, in most cases, it disappears after a day or a week at the longest, so we need to record proof. According to quick examination, the powder has identical properties as gold, but it has never lasted more than a week; it soon disappears.

This is how the spiritual energy of the heavenly world materializes in this world. Such phenomena do occur when spirits in the higher dimensional worlds above the fourth dimension try to make them happen on earth.

An example of a miracle:
Atopic dermatitis cured by revelations of a past life

Another miracle other than the gold powder phenomenon is the curing of illnesses. Cancer, for example, is one of the three major diseases; it reportedly accounts for a third of the causes of death for males, but even cancer can disappear.

A cancer tumor the size of a fist was found in one of our members during a hospital checkup, but after he took kigans (ritual prayers) at various shojas (temples) of Happy Science, it was found that the tumor had completely disappeared at his next medical examination. There are many reports like this at Happy Science.

There are also heart diseases. Western-style eating habits have increased the number of heart-related illnesses but there have been many reports of these being cured as well. In addition, other incurable and strange illnesses that cannot be explained or treated by modern medicine are also being healed at Happy Science. This is quite mysterious.

For example, there are ailments of the skin such as eczema. There was a man who developed atopic dermatitis all over his body when his skin was exposed to the sun. As a result, he could not go out in sunlight. He came to a lecture of mine at Hakone Shoja and asked me during the Q&A session how he could heal his skin problem. So I did a spiritual reading on him.

Non-believers of Happy Science may laugh, but I have been conducting numerous "space people readings," which are spiritual readings of those who have experienced lives on other planets before being born as a human on earth. There are many with such histories of their souls. I believe that the number of these cases proves that they are indeed true stories. In the case of this person, I did a spiritual reading on him to investigate his past experiences. I did not expect it to be a "space people reading," but I discovered that this person had once lived on Mars.

Mars, when in sunlight, has very high surface temperatures, and when in darkness becomes very cold. Therefore, some of the beings that existed there would live underground in fear of sunlight. So, I answered his question on the spot saying, "You had a past life where you avoided the sunlight, and because your soul remembers it, I guess your skin temperature goes up in the sunlight. That is why you develop atopic dermatitis when you go out in the sun." I said this regardless of whether he believed it or not, but in less than a month, his eczema was completely cured.

Illness disappears
When the patient becomes aware of the true cause

There are many cases like this outside Happy Science as well. In psychotherapy, for example, there is a treatment called hypnotic regression. This process tries to find the cause of a symptom by bringing back forgotten childhood memories that affect the person in the present, although they may be unaware of it.

Some patients regress to the time before birth and remember passing through the mother's birth canal or being in the mother's womb. Some even go far back to talk about life in the heavenly world or a previous life. It is reported that there is a certain percentage of people who speak about such things. Even if such memories are retained, in most cases, they only last until the person is five years old or so. By the time the child enters elementary school, memories begin to fade and are replaced by knowledge and experience gained in this world.

People have various past lives, and many of them now have illnesses that arise due to some specific experience in a past life. Therefore, people who suffer illnesses with unknown reasons or who suffer strange, incurable diseases may often discover the cause by having past life readings. Then, strangely enough, when the cause of the illness is found out, the "manifestation of the karma" breaks down and the illness starts to heal. This phenomenon is also found in regression therapy. The illness disappears when the person becomes aware of the cause.

It is truly a wonder. This may sound truly mysterious, but when the person understands the true cause, the illness starts to disintegrate and eventually disappears. I believe a great number of people will experience similar miracles from now on.

4

The World is Filled with Great Miracles

✧   ✧   ✧

Record miraculous phenomena
Like the healing of an illness

If I do a spiritual reading directly on someone, that person will know the exact cause of any illness but even if I am not present, one can go to any of the Happy Science shojas around the world and attend a meditation seminar or other seminars to find the cause for oneself. During a seminar, one can have various spiritual experiences: One may recall a past life and see it in a vision, find the root cause of their illness in a meditative state, or hear the voice of their guardian spirit. I believe many such things will continue to happen in great numbers.

So I will request in advance: Please keep a record of any miraculous phenomenon, such as an illness being cured (A documentary film, *Kiseki-tono-Deai* [lit. *An Encounter with Miracles*] – *Heart to Heart 3* – [original concept by Ryuho Okawa] is scheduled to be released in August 2020 in Japan). Although we may tend to take them for granted, miracles that happen at Happy Science and are reported in our publications are the kinds that truly amaze doctors. They might say, "Did I make a mistake? Did the X-ray machine malfunction?" Things that are not supposed to happen have been happening. There are many cases of illnesses being healed.

Everyone has the ability to heal illness themselves

I have never proactively made a declaration to cure illnesses; they just heal on their own. Japan has a strict law called the Medical Practitioners' Act so we cannot openly say we can cure illness; I will just say that illnesses heal on their own. There is no problem in curing an illness on your own by taking part in a kigan ceremony.

I recommend that you go to the Happy Science shojas or local temples and attend a koan seminar, practice meditation, pray, or participate in a lecture seminar and try to find the root cause of your physical disorder and heal it yourself. I say this because people innately have the power to heal their own illnesses.

As I have written in other books, a human being is the Light itself that comes from God and Buddha. Some have more Light than others; some are called the Light of Great Guiding Spirits or Archangels who have a responsibility to fulfill a grand mission. This is the truth. Not everyone has such a grand mission, but at least everyone is endowed with a soul. This is also a miracle.

Some people say that humans are like machines; physical bodies function as machines and finally break down after several dozen years. This is probably the usual, common way of thinking. But in fact, thank goodness, there is a soul in our physical bodies. Our souls have memories of the many lives we have lived in the past. Our souls are connected to such old memories. This is, in fact, a great miracle.

There is a meaning to all the experiences Of your 30,000-day life

Your soul is the real you, and your life in the heavenly world, or the Real World, is your true life. The life you spend in this world for about 30,000 days is your experience in the "school of the soul." You were born into this world to accumulate experiences for your soul. I want you to know this. Once you know it, you will be able to understand that your experiences in life, including the various kinds of suffering, difficulties, illnesses, failure in business, and setbacks in human relations, all have a meaning.

In the heavenly world, you live as a soul in a realm which accords with the level of your enlightenment, so your experience is limited as long as you live among those of a similar level of awareness as yours. In this world, on the other hand, you can accumulate new experiences. You can meet different kinds of people, whose original abodes in heaven are unknown. The person sitting in front of you may, in fact, be flapping giant angel wings, but since the wings are not visible in this world, you would have no idea about the person.

The existence of the God Ame-no-Mioya-Gami *At the root of Japanese Shinto*

Some people can see part of my spiritual figure during my public lectures. In the late 1980s, for instance, I heard that a child attending my lecture saw me in the form of a great statue of Buddha walking to the podium; I was so large that only my legs were visible, as the rest of my body stood through the ceiling. The lecture on that day was held at Ryogoku Kokugikan arena, a venue famous for sumo tournaments, and maybe the child saw me as a sumo wrestler. When I heard that, I could not believe it straightaway and it left me with mixed feelings.

However, recently, we discovered that the child's comment was not mistaken. Our "space people readings" revealed that the oldest God of Japanese Shinto was *Ame-no-Mioya-Gami*. We came to know that a very long time ago, the God Ame-no-Mioya-Gami led a large UFO fleet with around 200,000 humanoids from the Andromeda Galaxy and set down at the foot of Mt. Fuji in Japan. When we asked about the figure of the oldest and greatest God Ame-no-Mioya-Gami, to our surprise, He was a 25-m (80-ft) tall sumo-wrestler-like Being.

I was so surprised that Japan's sumo wrestling had such an ancient origin. It made me wonder about many things, including whether some food shortage caused humans to shrink to our current size. It seems that sumo has existed from the very origin of the Japanese Shinto religion. It was also confirmed that the customs of Shinto religion, such as putting one's hands together in prayer and bowing, have existed from that time.

Encountering your true self, soul mates, And a fantastic world

I have touched on various topics. We are now discovering that the world is far bigger than what we have learned through school education, and that it is filled with miracles. With such awareness, if you can grasp who you truly are, you will be able to achieve things you previously thought were impossible. It will be possible when you break out of your own "shell."

Up until then, you may only be able to perceive yourself as a human in a body, but you will begin to see a different self—for example, the self that once lived in the heavenly world, the self that has soul siblings, or how you have incarnated time and again from the other world to this one, and find your soul mates in this world.

This world is truly fantastic. From now on, new evidence will come out, one after another, to show that it is such a world that has been created. The very fact that we are living on earth will feel like we are living in a time of magic.

Those who have grasped and understood the Truth Will no longer fear death

Even if illnesses are healed, life will eventually come to an end, and you will have to leave this world. But those who have grasped and understood the Truth will find that even death is not something to fear.

Those who must be most fearful are those who lived their lives without ever thinking about what would happen to them after death. Even if people have lived without giving it any thought, those who lived a good life will certainly have a chance to be saved. But severe hardship awaits those who believed their lives were limited to this world only to find there was actually more, realizing too late how wrongfully they had lived.

This is a simple truth. You may have heard it a lot in folktales. Some may have considered it a mere parable. Even among notable scholars, many probably regard it as mere metaphor. Some studying Buddhism describe only that which adheres to common sense in this world and remove all spiritual aspects. Some Christians, though they say they believe in Christianity, only learn sections from the Bible that do not contain any miraculous elements.

But there is more to this world than what seems sensible. Miracles exist in all ages. Please be aware that all people are living through a time filled with miracles.

5
The Power to Make Miracles
And to Change the World

✦   ✦   ✦

Be aware of a far greater power than before

While living as a human, you may sometimes face hardships. If not hardships, you will experience difficult times as you struggle to achieve some high goals you set for yourself. But in your subconscious, you have a great power hidden within you, far greater than you think you now have. When you become aware of this, you can transform into a different person.

You will realize that what appears to be sorrow or suffering has actually been just a sandpaper to refine your soul. You will also be able to advance in your enlightenment and raise your awareness much higher than you expected.

Live with a transparent heart

Then, what is the state of mind that you are expected to achieve in the end? Let me explain it simply.

The first point is this: Try to live as purely as possible. It may sound silly to live with a pure heart in this world. Some may say it would not make you any money. Many may argue that if we live with a pure heart, we will only be deceived, mocked, or lose in this world. But these are not what I mean.

By living purely, your heart will become transparent, and when your heart is transparent, you will be able to see what you could not see before. You will be attuned to the spirits in heaven and be able to see other people of Light living in this world with you.

To keep your heart pure and transparent, you need to clear away any "rust" or "dust" from your mind every day. This will be an important discipline.

Do not consider it lightly, though it is a simple practice. At the end of the day, look back and see if you have lacked in any effort, made too harsh a remark to others, hurt someone or caused some trouble. If you have found any mistakes, reflect on them one by one and clear away any negativity. This practice of self-reflection will polish your heart; as if wiping the surface of a mirror, your heart will gradually be transparent.

Then, light from heaven will start to flow into you. This light will make miracles, multiplying your power to live twofold or even tenfold. This is the first point I ask of you.

Live with love

The second point is this: Try to live with love while you live as a human being. This may sound naive and superficial, but if the whole of humanity, each and every person, makes an effort to live with love, this world will move forward in a better direction little by little. The world can only get better.

There are differences in nationality, race, and religion. Our ways of thinking and beliefs also differ. It is natural. There is variety in human living as we have different occupations. There are many other differences and not everyone has the same ideas, but we were born into this world all knowing this fact. We are expected to live some dozens of years of life together with many others who have different ways of thinking while working hard and refining our souls with each other. Therefore, we must go beyond our differences and overcome difficult obstacles to create an age where all people can live together. This is important.

In a simple word, it is called "love." Love is misunderstood in modern society. It often becomes "love that takes" or love that you expect to receive, and when you fail to get love, you often feel sad or want to somehow take revenge. But when more people practice giving love, this world will definitely get closer to a utopia.

You may have other desires, such as getting a pay raise, improving your relations, or climbing the ladder of success at work, but these things will follow later. Before anything else, make efforts to create a world of "giving love." It does not cost a cent to do this. You just need to turn on the small generator in your heart and pray, "Let me be of service to others, even if a little," "Let me be a kind person," or "May that person's life get better."

From love to prayer

Sometimes your prayer may not be realized, but if your prayer is a genuine act of love, then that act of love is immortal. It will never disappear. It will forever be recorded in your soul.

So, let us do what we must in this world. One's greatness is determined by their actions. One's actions determine their true status, position, and greatness.

What is more, pray. "From love to prayer"—this will open up the future even more. Some prayers are yet to be realized, but if many people come together and pray, the world will move in that direction. To create such a world, let us continue working together.

AFTERWORD

You need to go through difficulties and trials to establish true faith, just like a sword that is tempered in fire and water when forged.

To fulfill *noblesse oblige*, sometimes you need to abandon fame, social position, property, personal relations or even family and maintain a detached state of mind.

Overcome your many failures and keep disciplining yourself to the fullest without relying on miracles. There is a rainbow only those who have gone through such experience can see.

Between love and attachments, how hard it is to live each day with a calm mind.

Be a person of steel. With resilience and a focused mind, defeat darkness. Never expect that you can harvest all fruits in this lifetime alone.

Ryuho Okawa
Master and CEO of Happy Science Group
December 2019

This book is a compilation of the lectures, with additions, as listed below.

- Chapter One -   The Mindset to Invite Prosperity
Japanese title: *Han'ei wo Maneku tameno Kangaekata*
Lecture given on November 23, 2018
at Special Lecture Hall, Happy Science, Tokyo, Japan

- Chapter Two -   The Law of Cause and Effect
Japanese title: *Gen'in to Kekka no Housoku*
Lecture given on November 14, 2018
at Happy Science General Headquarters, Tokyo, Japan

- Chapter Three -   Fulfilling *Noblesse Oblige*
Japanese title: *Kouki naru Gimu wo Hatasu tameni*
Lecture given on May 3, 2018
at Tokyo Shoshinkan, Happy Science, Tokyo, Japan

- Chapter Four -   Be Confident in Your Life
Japanese title: *Jinsei ni Jishin wo Mote*
Lecture given on July 5, 2019
at Fukuoka Kokusai Center, Fukuoka, Japan

- Chapter Five -   A Savior's Wish
Japanese title: *Kyuseishu no Negai*
Lecture given on April 29, 2019
at Special Lecture Hall, Happy Science, Tokyo, Japan

- Chapter Six -   The Power to Make Miracles
Japanese title: *Kiseki wo Okosu Chikara*
Lecture given on December 11, 2018
at Makuhari Messe International Exhibition Hall, Chiba, Japan

Life-Changing Words are quoted from the books and the lectures listed below.

- Life-Changing Words 1 - Thoughts Will Generate Extremely Strong Power
Japanese title: *Kangaekata wa Hijou ni Tsuyoi Chikara wo umu*
Quoted from: "Fukyo wo Norikoeru tameno Kihonteki na Kangaekata"
(literally, "The essential ways of thinking to overcome recession") in Chapter
One of *Chie no Keiei* (literally, "Management with Wisdom")

- Life-Changing Words 2 - In Hardships, Gain Brilliance of the Soul and Virtue
Japanese title: *Shiren no naka de Tamashii no Kagayaki to Toku wo eru*
Quoted from: Chapter Five "The Power of the Strong Mind" of *The Strong
Mind* (New York: IRH Press, 2018)

- Life-Changing Words 3 - A Small Enlightenment that Leads Individuals and
Organizations to Success
Japanese title: *Kojin mo Soshiki mo Seikou saseru "Chiisana Satori"*
Quoted from: "Keiei ga Kuroji dearu koto no Chiisana Yorokobi" (literally,
"The small joy that your company is in the black") in Chapter Two of *Keiei to
Jinbo-ryoku* (literally, "Management and Admirable Qualities")

- Life-Changing Words 4 - Message from El Cantare, God of the Earth
Japanese title: *Chikyushin El Cantare karano Message*
Quoted from: Chapter Six "The Choice of Humankind" of *The Laws of Faith*
(New York: IRH Press, 2018)

- Life-Changing Words 5 - Abandon, If You Want to Protect
Japanese title: *Mamoran to sureba Suteyo*
Quoted from: Chapter Five "Have a Stronger Faith" of *My Lover, Cross the
Valley of Tears* (Tokyo: Happy Science, 2008)

ABOUT THE AUTHOR

RYUHO OKAWA was born on July 7th 1956, in Tokushima, Japan. After graduating from the University of Tokyo with a law degree, he joined a Tokyo-based trading house. While working at its New York headquarters, he studied international finance at the Graduate Center of the City University of New York. In 1981, he attained Great Enlightenment and became aware that he is El Cantare with a mission to bring salvation to all of humankind. In 1986 he established Happy Science. It now has members in over 100 countries across the world, with more than 700 local branches and temples as well as 10,000 missionary houses around the world. The total number of lectures has exceeded 3,100 (of which more than 150 are in English) and over 2,600 books (of which more than 500 are Spiritual Interview Series) have been published, many of which are translated into 31 languages. Many of the books, including *The Laws of the Sun* have become best sellers or million sellers. To date, Happy Science has produced 20 movies. The original story and original concept were given by the Executive Producer Ryuho Okawa. Recent movie titles are *The Real Exorcist* (live-action movie released in May 2020), *Kiseki to no Deai - Kokoro ni Yorisou 3 -* (lit. "Encounters with Miracles - Heart to Heart 3 -," documentary scheduled to be released in Aug. 2020), and *Twiceborn* (live-action movie to be released in Fall of 2020). He has also composed the lyrics and music of over 100 songs, such as theme songs and featured songs of movies. Moreover, he is the Founder of Happy Science University and Happy Science Academy (Junior and Senior High School), Founder and President of the Happiness Realization Party, Founder and Honorary Headmaster of Happy Science Institute of Government and Management, Founder of IRH Press Co., Ltd., and the Chairperson of New Star Production Co., Ltd. and ARI Production Co., Ltd.

WHAT IS EL CANTARE?

El Cantare means "the Light of the Earth," and is the Supreme God of the Earth who has been guiding humankind since the beginning of Genesis. He is whom Jesus called Father. Different parts of El Cantare's core consciousness have descended to Earth in the past, once as Alpha and another as Elohim. His branch spirits, such as Shakyamuni Buddha and Hermes, have descended to Earth many times and helped to flourish many civilizations. To unite various religions and to integrate various fields of study in order to build a new civilization on Earth, a part of the core consciousness has descended to Earth as Master Ryuho Okawa.

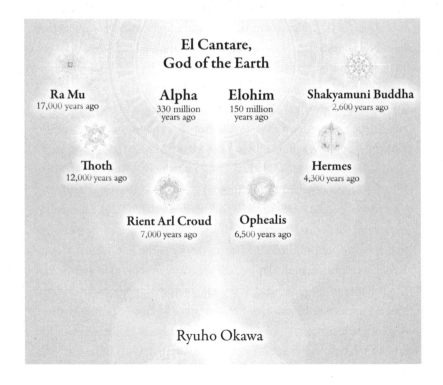

**El Cantare,
God of the Earth**

Ra Mu
17,000 years ago

Alpha
330 million
years ago

Elohim
150 million
years ago

Shakyamuni Buddha
2,600 years ago

Thoth
12,000 years ago

Hermes
4,300 years ago

Rient Arl Croud
7,000 years ago

Ophealis
6,500 years ago

Ryuho Okawa

Alpha Alpha is a part of the core consciousness of El Cantare that descended to Earth more than 300 million years ago. Alpha preached Earth's Truths to harmonize and unify Earth-born humans and space people who came from other planets.

Elohim Elohim is the name of El Cantare's core consciousness that lived on Earth 150 million years ago. He taught teachings of wisdom, mainly on the differences of light and darkness, good and evil.

Shakyamuni Buddha Gautama Siddhartha was born as a prince into the Shakya Clan in India around 2,600 years ago. When he was 29 years old, he renounced the world and sought enlightenment. He later attained Great Enlightenment and founded Buddhism.

Hermes In the Greek mythology, Hermes is thought of as one of the 12 Olympian gods, but the spiritual Truth is that he taught the teachings of love and progress around 4,300 years ago that became the origin of the current Western civilization. He is a hero that truly existed.

Ophealis Ophealis was born in Greece around 6,500 years ago and was the leader who took an expedition to as far as Egypt. He is the God of miracles, prosperity, and arts, and is known as Osiris in the Egyptian mythology.

Rient Arl Croud Rient Arl Croud was born as a king of the ancient Incan Empire around 7,000 years ago and taught about the mysteries of the mind. In the heavenly world, he is responsible for the interactions that take place between various planets.

Thoth Thoth was an almighty leader who built the golden age of the Atlantic civilization around 12,000 years ago. In the Egyptian mythology, he is known as god Thoth.

Ra Mu Ra Mu was a leader who built the golden age of the civilization of Mu around 17,000 years ago. As a religious leader and a politician, he ruled by uniting religion and politics.

WHAT IS A SPIRITUAL MESSAGE?

We are all spiritual beings living on this earth. The following is the mechanism behind Ryuho Okawa's spiritual messages.

1 You are a spirit

People are born into this world to gain wisdom through various experiences and return to the other world when their lives end. We are all spirits and repeat this cycle in order to refine our souls.

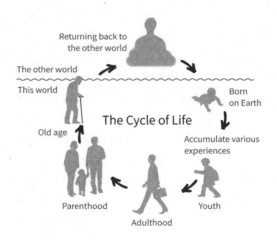

Returning back to the other world

The other world

This world

Born on Earth

The Cycle of Life

Old age

Accumulate various experiences

Parenthood

Adulthood

Youth

2 You have a guardian spirit

Guardian spirits are those who protect the people living on this earth. Each of us has a guardian spirit that watches over us and guides us from the other world. They are one of our past lives, and are identical in how we think.

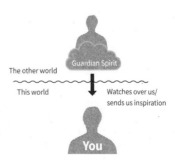

The other world

Guardian Spirit

This world

Watches over us/ sends us inspiration

You

3 How spiritual messages work

Since a guardian spirit thinks at the same subconscious level as the person living on earth, Ryuho Okawa can summon the spirit and find out what the person on earth is actually thinking. If the person has already returned to the other world, the spirit can give messages to the people living on earth through Ryuho Okawa.

1 The guardian spirit / spirit in the other world...

2 Goes inside Ryuho Okawa in this world

3 Okawa speaks the words of the guardian spirit / spirit

The spiritual messages of more than 1,000 sessions have been openly recorded by Ryuho Okawa since 2009, and the majority of these have been published. Spiritual messages from the guardian spirits of living politicians such as U.S. President Trump, Japanese Prime Minister Shinzo Abe and Chinese President Xi Jinping, as well as spiritual messages sent from the Spirit World by Jesus Christ, Muhammad, Thomas Edison, Mother Teresa, Steve Jobs and Nelson Mandela are just a tiny pack of spiritual messages that were published so far.

Domestically, in Japan, these spiritual messages are being read by a wide range of politicians and mass media, and the high-level contents of these books are delivering an impact even more on politics, news and public opinion. In recent years, there have been spiritual messages recorded in English, and English translations are being done on the spiritual messages given in Japanese. These have been published overseas, one after another, and have started to shake the world.

For more about spiritual messages and a complete list of books, visit **okawabooks.com**

ABOUT HAPPY SCIENCE

Happy Science is a global movement that empowers individuals to find purpose and spiritual happiness and to share that happiness with their families, societies, and the world. With more than twelve million members around the world, Happy Science aims to increase awareness of spiritual truths and expand our capacity for love, compassion, and joy so that together we can create the kind of world we all wish to live in.

Activities at Happy Science are based on the Principles of Happiness (Love, Wisdom, Self-Reflection, and Progress). These principles embrace worldwide philosophies and beliefs, transcending boundaries of culture and religions.

Love teaches us to give ourselves freely without expecting anything in return; it encompasses giving, nurturing, and forgiving.

Wisdom leads us to the insights of spiritual truths, and opens us to the true meaning of life and the will of God (the universe, the highest power, Buddha).

Self-Reflection brings a mindful, nonjudgmental lens to our thoughts and actions to help us find our truest selves—the essence of our souls—and deepen our connection to the highest power. It helps us attain a clean and peaceful mind and leads us to the right life path.

Progress emphasizes the positive, dynamic aspects of our spiritual growth—actions we can take to manifest and spread happiness around the world. It's a path that not only expands our soul growth, but also furthers the collective potential of the world we live in.

PROGRAMS AND EVENTS

The doors of Happy Science are open to all. We offer a variety of programs and events, including self-exploration and self-growth programs, spiritual seminars, meditation and contemplation sessions, study groups, and book events.

Our programs are designed to:
* Deepen your understanding of your purpose and meaning in life
* Improve your relationships and increase your capacity to love unconditionally
* Attain peace of mind, decrease anxiety and stress, and feel positive
* Gain deeper insights and a broader perspective on the world
* Learn how to overcome life's challenges
  ... and much more.

*For more information, visit **happy-science.org**.*

INTERNATIONAL SEMINARS

Each year, friends from all over the world join our international seminars, held at our faith centers in Japan. Different programs are offered each year and cover a wide variety of topics, including improving relationships, practicing the Eightfold Path to enlightenment, and loving yourself, to name just a few.

HAPPY SCIENCE MONTHLY

Happy Science regularly publishes various magazines for readers around the world. The Happy Science Monthly, which now spans over 300 issues, contains Master Okawa's latest lectures, words of wisdom, stories of remarkable life-changing experiences, world news, and much more to guide members and their friends to a happier life. This is available in many other languages, including Portuguese, Spanish, French, German, Chinese, and Korean. Happy Science Basics, on the other hand, is a 'theme-based' booklet made in an easy-to-read style for those new to Happy Science, which is also ideal to give to friends and family. You can pick up the latest issues from Happy Science, subscribe to have them delivered (see our contacts page) or view them online.*

* Online editions of the *Happy Science Monthly* and *Happy Science Basics* can be viewed at:
info.happy-science.org/category/magazines/

CONTACT INFORMATION

Happy Science is a worldwide organization with faith centers around the globe. For a comprehensive list of centers, visit the worldwide directory at *happy-science.org*. The following are some of the many Happy Science locations:

UNITED STATES AND CANADA

New York
79 Franklin St., New York, NY 10013
Phone: 212-343-7972
Fax: 212-343-7973
Email: ny@happy-science.org
Website: happyscience-na.org

San Francisco
525 Clinton St.
Redwood City, CA 94062
Phone & Fax: 650-363-2777
Email: sf@happy-science,org
Website: happyscience-na.org

New Jersey
725 River Rd, #102B, Edgewater, NJ 07020
Phone: 201-313-0127
Fax: 201-313-0120
Email: nj@happy-science.org
Website: happyscience-na.org

Los Angeles
1590 E. Del Mar Blvd., Pasadena, CA 91106
Phone: 626-395-7775
Fax: 626-395-7776
Email: la@happy-science.org
Website: happyscience-na.org

Florida
5208 8th St., St. Zephyrhills, FL 33542
Phone: 813-715-0000
Fax: 813-715-0010
Email: florida@happy-science.org
Website: happyscience-na.org

Orange County
10231 Slater Ave., #204
Fountain Valley, CA 92708
Phone: 714-745-1140
Email: oc@happy-science.org
Website: happyscience-na.org

Atlanta
1874 Piedmont Ave., NE Suite 360-C
Atlanta, GA 30324
Phone: 404-892-7770
Email: atlanta@happy-science.org
Website: happyscience-na.org

San Diego
7841 Balboa Ave., Suite #202
San Diego, CA 92111
Phone: 619-381-7615
Fax: 626-395-7776
E-mail: sandiego@happy-science.org
Website: happyscience-na.org

Hawaii
Phone: 808-591-9772
Fax: 808-591-9776
Email: hi@happy-science.org
Website: happyscience-na.org

Toronto
845 The Queensway
Etobicoke ON M8Z 1N6 Canada
Phone: 1-416-901-3747
Email: toronto@happy-science.org
Website: happy-science.ca

Kauai
3343 Kanakolu Street, Suite 5
Lihue, HI 96766, U.S.A.
Phone: 808-822-7007
Fax: 808-822-6007
Email: kauai-hi@happy-science.org
Website: kauai.happyscience-na.org

Vancouver
#201-2607 East 49th Avenue
Vancouver, BC, V5S 1J9, Canada
Phone: 1-604-437-7735
Fax: 1-604-437-7764
Email: vancouver@happy-science.org
Website: happy-science.ca

INTERNATIONAL

Tokyo
1-6-7 Togoshi, Shinagawa
Tokyo, 142-0041 Japan
Phone: 81-3-6384-5770
Fax: 81-3-6384-5776
Email: tokyo@happy-science.org
Website: happy-science.org

Seoul
74, Sadang-ro 27-gil,
Dongjak-gu, Seoul, Korea
Phone: 82-2-3478-8777
Fax: 82-2-3478-9777
Email: korea@happy-science.org
Website: happyscience-korea.org

London
3 Margaret St.
London,W1W 8RE United Kingdom
Phone: 44-20-7323-9255
Fax: 44-20-7323-9344
Email: eu@happy-science.org
Website: happyscience-uk.org

Brazil Headquarters
Rua. Domingos de Morais 1154,
Vila Mariana, Sao Paulo SP
CEP 04009-002, Brazil
Phone: 55-11-5088-3800
Fax: 55-11-5088-3806
Email: sp@happy-science.org
Website: happyscience.com.br

Sydney
516 Pacific Hwy, Lane Cove North,
NSW 2066, Australia
Phone: 61-2-9411-2877
Fax: 61-2-9411-2822
Email: sydney@happy-science.org

Jundiai
Rua Congo, 447, Jd. Bonfiglioli
Jundiai-CEP, 13207-340
Phone: 55-11-4587-5952
Email: jundiai@happy-science.org

Taipei

No. 89, Lane 155, Dunhua N. Road
Songshan District, Taipei City 105, Taiwan
Phone: 886-2-2719-9377
Fax: 886-2-2719-5570
Email: taiwan@happy-science.org
Website: happyscience-tw.org

Thailand

19 Soi Sukhumvit 60/1,
Bang Chak, Phra Khanong,
Bangkok, 10260 Thailand
Phone: 66-2-007-1419
Email: bangkok@happy-science.org
Website: happyscience-thai.org

Malaysia

No 22A, Block 2, Jalil Link Jalan Jalil Jaya 2,
Bukit Jalil 57000, Kuala Lumpur, Malaysia
Phone: 60-3-8998-7877
Fax: 60-3-8998-7977
Email: malaysia@happy-science.org
Website: happyscience.org.my

Indonesia

Darmawangsa
Square Lt. 2 No. 225
Jl. Darmawangsa VI & IX
Indonesia
Phone: 021-7278-0756
Email: indonesia@happy-science.org

Nepal

Kathmandu Metropolitan City Ward No. 15,
Ring Road, Kimdol,
Sitapaila Kathmandu, Nepal
Phone: 97-714-272931
Email: nepal@happy-science.org

Philippines Taytay

LGL Bldg, 2nd Floor,
Kadalagaham cor,
Rizal Ave. Taytay,
Rizal, Philippines
Phone: 63-2-5710686
Email: philippines@happy-science.org

Uganda

Plot 877 Rubaga Road, Kampala
P.O. Box 34130, Kampala, Uganda
Phone: 256-79-3238-002
Email: uganda@happy-science.org
Website: happyscience-uganda.org

SOCIAL CONTRIBUTIONS

Happy Science tackles social issues such as suicide and bullying, and launches heartfelt, precise and prompt rescue operations after a major disaster.

◆ The HS Nelson Mandela Fund

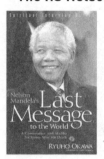

The Happy Science Group provides disaster relief and educational aid overseas via this Fund. We established it following the publication of *Nelson Mandela's Last Message to the World*, a spiritual message from the late Nelson Mandela, in 2013. The fund actively provides both material and spiritual aid to people overseas—support for victims of racial discrimination, poverty, political oppression, natural disasters, and more.

Examples of how the fund has been used:

Provided tents in rural Nepal

Supplied food and water immediately after the Nepal earthquake

Donated a container library to South African primary school, in collaboration with Nelson Mandela Foundation

◆ **We extend a helping hand around the world to aid in post-disaster reconstruction and education.**

NEPAL: After the 2015 Nepal Earthquake, we promptly offered our local temple as a temporary evacuation center and utilized our global network to send water, food and tents. We will keep supporting their recovery via the HS Nelson Mandela Fund.

SRI LANKA: Provided aid in constructing school buildings damaged by the tsunami. Further, with the help of the Sri Lankan prime minister, 100 bookshelves were donated to Buddhist temples.

INDIA: Ongoing aid since 2006—uniforms, school meals, etc. for schools in Bodh Gaya, a sacred ground for Buddhism. Medical aid in Calcutta, in collaboration with local hospitals.

CHINA: Donated money and tents to the Szechuan Earthquake disaster zone. Books were also donated to elementary schools in Gansu Province, near the disaster zone.

UGANDA: Donated educational materials and mosquito nets to protect children from Malaria. Donated a school building and prayer hall to a private secondary school, as well as offering a scholarship to a university student who had graduated from the school.

GHANA: Provided medical supplies as a preventive measure against Ebola.

SOUTH AFRICA: Collaborated with the Nelson Mandela Foundation in South Africa to donate a container library and books to an elementary school.

IRAN: Donated to the earthquake-stricken area in northeastern Iran in October 2012 via the Iranian Embassy.

HAPPINESS REALIZATION PARTY

The Happiness Realization Party (HRP) was founded in May 2009 by Master Ryuho Okawa as part of the Happy Science Group to offer concrete and proactive solutions to the current issues such as military threats from North Korea and China and the long-term economic recession. HRP aims to implement drastic reforms of the Japanese government, thereby bringing peace and prosperity to Japan. To accomplish this, HRP proposes two key policies:

1) Strengthening the national security and the Japan-U.S. alliance which plays a vital role in the stability of Asia.

2) Improving the Japanese economy by implementing drastic tax cuts, taking monetary easing measures and creating new major industries.

HRP advocates that Japan should offer a model of a religious nation that allows diverse values and beliefs to coexist, and that contributes to global peace.

*For more information, visit **en.hr-party.jp***

HAPPY SCIENCE ACADEMY JUNIOR AND SENIOR HIGH SCHOOL

Happy Science Academy Junior and Senior High School is a boarding school founded with the goal of educating the future leaders of the world who can have a big vision, persevere, and take on new challenges.

Currently, there are two campuses in Japan; the Nasu Main Campus in Tochigi Prefecture, founded in 2010, and the Kansai Campus in Shiga Prefecture, founded in 2013.

Nasu Main Campus

Kansai Campus

HAPPY SCIENCE UNIVERSITY

THE FOUNDING SPIRIT AND THE GOAL OF EDUCATION

Based on the founding philosophy of the university, "Exploration of happiness and the creation of a new civilization," education, research and studies will be provided to help students acquire deep understanding grounded in religious belief and advanced expertise with the objectives of producing "great talents of virtue" who can contribute in a broad-ranging way to serve Japan and the international society.

FACULTIES

Faculty of Human Happiness

Students in this faculty will pursue liberal arts from various perspectives with a multidisciplinary approach, explore and envision an ideal state of human beings and society.

Faculty of Successful Management

This faculty aims to realize successful management that helps organizations to create value and wealth for society and to contribute to the happiness and the development of management and employees as well as society as a whole.

Faculty of Future Creation

Students in this faculty study subjects such as political science, journalism, performing arts and artistic expression, and explore and present new political and cultural models based on truth, goodness and beauty.

Faculty of Future Industry

This faculty aims to nurture engineers who can resolve various issues facing modern civilization from a technological standpoint and contribute to the creation of new industries of the future.

THE REAL EXORCIST

STORY Tokyo —the most mystical city in the world where you find spiritual spots in the most unexpected places. Sayuri works as a part time waitress at a small coffee shop "Extra" where regular customers enjoy the authentic coffee that the owner brews. Meanwhile, Sayuri uses her supernatural powers to help those who are troubled by spiritual phenomena one after another. Through her special consultations, she touches the hearts of the people and helps them by showing the truths of the invisible world.

BEST FEATURE FILM
17ᵗʰ Angel Film Awards
2020
Monaco International Film Festival

BEST FEMALE ACTOR
17ᵗʰ Angel Film Awards
2020
Monaco International Film Festival

BEST FEMALE SUPPORTING ACTOR
17ᵗʰ Angel Film Awards
2020
Monaco International Film Festival

BEST VISUAL EFFECTS
17ᵗʰ Angel Film Awards
2020
Monaco International Film Festival

BEST FEATURE FILM
EKO International Film Festival
2020

BEST SUPPORTING ACTRESS
EKO International Film Festival
2020

For more information, visit ___www.realexorcistmovie.com___

ABOUT IRH PRESS USA

IRH Press USA Inc. was founded in 2013 as an affiliated firm of IRH Press Co., Ltd. Based in New York, the press publishes books in various categories including spirituality, religion, and self-improvement and publishes books by Ryuho Okawa, the author of over 100 million books sold worldwide. For more information, visit *okawabooks.com*.

Follow us on:

Facebook: Okawa Books   **Twitter**: Okawa Books
Goodreads: Ryuho Okawa   **Instagram**: OkawaBooks
Pinterest: Okawa Books

RYUHO OKAWA'S LAWS SERIES

The Laws Series is an annual volume of books that are mainly comprised of Ryuho Okawa's lectures on various topics that highlight principles and guidelines for the activities of Happy Science every year. *The Laws of the Sun*, the first publication of the laws series, ranked in the annual best-selling list in Japan in 1987. Since then, all of the laws series' titles have ranked in the annual best-selling list for more than two decades, setting socio-cultural trends in Japan and around the world.

THE TRILOGY

The first three volumes of the Laws Series, *The Laws of the Sun*, *The Golden Laws*, and *The Nine Dimensions* make a trilogy that completes the basic framework of the teachings of God's Truths. *The Laws of the Sun* discusses the structure of God's Laws, *The Golden Laws* expounds on the doctrine of time, and *The Nine Dimensions* reveals the nature of space.

BOOKS BY RYUHO OKAWA

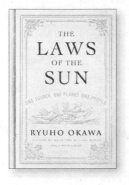

THE LAWS OF THE SUN
ONE SOURCE, ONE PLANET, ONE PEOPLE

Paperback • 288 pages • $15.95
ISBN: 978-1-942125-43-3

Imagine if you could ask God why he created this world and what spiritual laws he used to shape us—and everything around us. In *The Laws of the Sun*, Ryuho Okawa outlines these laws of the universe and provides a road map for living one's life with greater purpose and meaning. This powerful book shows the way to realize true happiness—a happiness that continues from this world through the other.

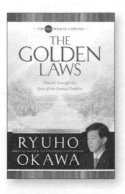

THE GOLDEN LAWS
HISTORY THROUGH THE EYES OF THE ETERNAL BUDDHA

Paperback • 201 pages • $14.95
ISBN: 978-1-941779-81-1

Throughout history, Great Guiding Spirits of Light have been present on Earth in both the East and the West at crucial points in human history to further our spiritual development. *The Golden Laws* reveals how Divine Plan has been unfolding on Earth, and outlines 5,000 years of the secret history of humankind.

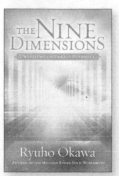

THE NINE DIMENSIONS
UNVEILING THE LAWS OF ETERNITY

Paperback • 168 pages • $15.95
ISBN: 978-0-982698-56-3

This book is a window into the mind of our loving God, who designed this world and the vast, wondrous world of our afterlife as a school with many levels through which our souls learn and grow. When the religions and cultures of the world discover the truth of their common spiritual origin, they will be inspired to accept their differences, come together under faith in God, and build an era of harmony and peaceful progress on Earth.

For a complete list of books, visit **okawabooks.com**

THE NEW RESURRECTION
MY MIRACULOUS STORY OF OVERCOMING ILLNESS AND DEATH

Hardcover • 224 pages • $19.95
ISBN: 978-1-942125-64-8

The New Resurrection is an autobiographical account of an astonishing miracle experienced by author Ryuho Okawa in 2004. This event was adapted into the feature-length film *Immortal Hero*, released in Japan, the United States and Canada during the Fall of 2019. Today, Okawa lives each day with the readiness to die for the Truth and has dedicated his life to selflessly guide faith seekers towards spiritual development and happiness. In testament to Okawa's earnest resolve, the appendix showcases a myriad of accomplishments by Okawa, chronicled after his miraculous resurrection.

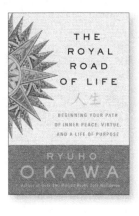

THE ROYAL ROAD OF LIFE
BEGINNING YOUR PATH OF INNER PEACE, VIRTUE, AND A LIFE OF PURPOSE

Paperback • 224 pages • $16.95
ISBN: 978-1-942125-53-2

With over 30 years of lectures and teachings spanning diverse topics of faith, self-growth, leadership (and more), Ryuho Okawa presents the profound eastern wisdom that he has cultivated on his approach to life. *The Royal Road of Life* illuminates a path to becoming a person of virtue, whose character and depth will move and inspire others towards the same meaningful destination.

---

*For a complete list of books, visit **okawabooks.com***

THE TRUMP SECRET

SEEING THROUGH THE PAST, PRESENT, AND FUTURE OF THE NEW AMERICAN PRESIDENT

Paperback • 208 pages • $14.95
ISBN: 978-1-942125-22-8

Donald Trump's victory in the 2016 presidential election surprised almost all major vote forecasters who predicted Hillary Clinton's victory. But 10 months earlier, in January 2016, Ryuho Okawa, Global Visionary, a renowned spiritual leader, and international best-selling author, had already foreseen Trump's victory. This book contains a series of lectures and interviews that unveil the secrets to Trump's victory and makes predictions of what will happen under his presidency. This book predicts the coming of a new America that will go through a great transformation from the "red and blue states" to the United States.

THE REASON WE ARE HERE

MAKE OUR POWERS TOGETHER TO REALIZE GOD'S JUSTICE -CHINA ISSUE, GLOBAL WARMING, AND LGBT-

Paperback • 215 pages • $14.95
ISBN: 978-1-943869-62-6

The Reason We Are Here is a book of thought that is unlike any other: its global perspective, timely opinion on current issues, and spiritual class are unmatched. The main content is the lecture in Toronto, Canada given in October 2019 by Ryuho Okawa, a Japanese spiritual leader and the national teacher of Japan. Also included are his answers to the questions—specifically, on the Hong Kong and Uyghur problems—from renowned activists who attended his lecture.

THE LAWS OF GREAT ENLIGHTENMENT
Always Walk with Buddha

LOVE FOR THE FUTURE
Building One World of Freedom and Democracy Under God's Truth

THE LAWS OF BRONZE
Love One Another, Become One People

THE LAWS OF INVINCIBLE LEADERSHIP
An Empowering Guide for Continuous and
Lasting Success in Business and in Life

THE STARTING POINT OF HAPPINESS
An Inspiring Guide to Positive Living with Faith, Love, and Courage

HEALING FROM WITHIN
Life-Changing Keys to Calm, Spiritual, and Healthy Living

THE UNHAPPINESS SYNDROME
28 Habits of Unhappy People (and How to Change Them)

THINK BIG!
Be Positive and Be Brave to Achieve Your Dreams

THE MOMENT OF TRUTH
Become a Living Angel Today

---

*For a complete list of books, visit **okawabooks.com***